OWN YOUR FINANCIAL FUTURE

TAKE CHARGE OF YOUR INVESTMENTS

PETER McMURTRY
B.COM, CFA

Own Your Financial Future: Take Charge of your Investments
© Peter McMurtry, 2021

ISBN: 978-1-7770835-1-9

Cover and Book Design: Clémence Palvadeau
Charts by permission YCharts

Peter McMurtry, B.Com, CFA
www.mcmurtryinvestmentreport.ca
Ottawa, ON, Canada

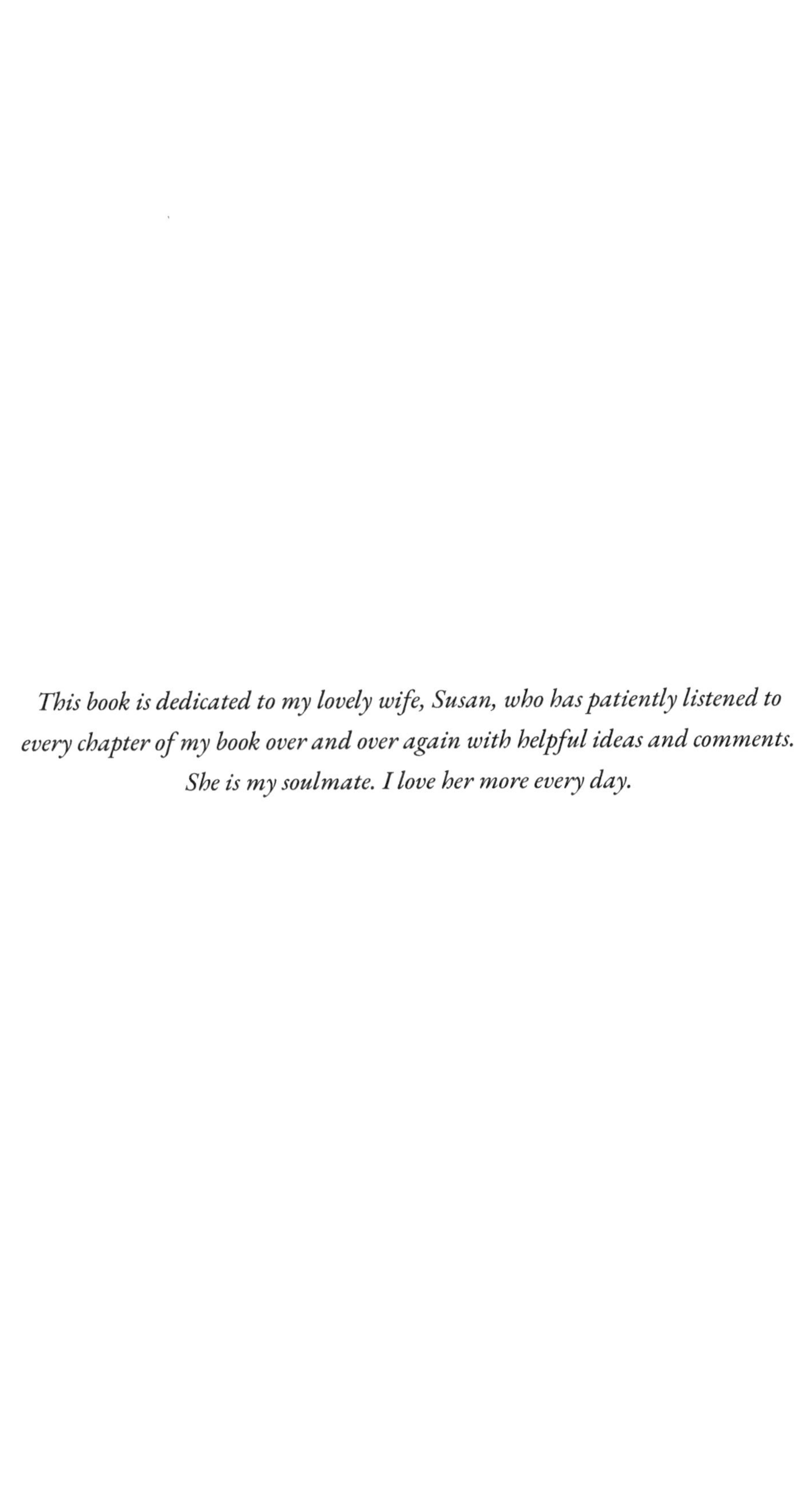

This book is dedicated to my lovely wife, Susan, who has patiently listened to every chapter of my book over and over again with helpful ideas and comments. She is my soulmate. I love her more every day.

CONTENTS

INTRODUCTION

Congratulations. You have taken the first steps to take charge of your financial affairs. As long as you remain totally committed, the opportunities are endless. Do not be intimidated at the task in front of you. It will all be worth it.

This book will provide you with the necessary tools to help lower the fees you pay, improving both the returns you receive and the consistency of those returns. Ensuring that more of your investment returns are put in your pocket, not your adviser's, is a good strategy for growing your net worth. I am offering experienced advice to help you manage your own investments without the burden of advisers who do not always have your best interests in mind. If you are not financially savvy you may believe that hiring someone to manage your investments is your only alternative. After my thirty-five years in this industry, I am fully cognizant of the fallacies of this ingrained belief.

Some of the tools in this book include how to set up and manage an investment portfolio, how to monitor and change your overall asset mix and how to select individual stocks for purchase and when to sell or reduce your current holdings. A specific chapter is devoted to how to read financial statements to ensure you have all the relevant information to make sound investment decisions. If you are not comfortable paying mutual fund management fees, there is a chapter summarizing how to liquidate your deferred sales charge funds without incurring excessive redemption charges. I have also included a chapter on how to position your investments at different stages of your life from working to retirement.

For many of us, including myself, who are not mechanically inclined, getting my car repaired is not a pleasant experience. Garages love clients like us as they can inflate the cost of repairs with little argument. We are the guinea pigs who are the bread and butter for the thousands of garages that fix our automobiles. Many of us have been told from a young age that it is usually more prudent to go to an expert rather than attempting to do it ourselves. However, I strongly disagree with this notion. I am not saying that we have to be experts in every field. What I mean is that it is always a good idea to be better informed, to seek a second opinion and to question your service provider.

This book summarizes where to find objective, unbiased financial information and explains how to use it to your advantage. You will still need to do your homework. There are no shortcuts to financial freedom, but there are plenty of ways to make your chances for success a lot better.

Recently, I have listened to many financial and investment advisers who downplay do-it-yourself investors as risky and uninformed. One told an audience that most individuals were not capable of doing it themselves as they did not have the financial savvy and years of experience under their belt. This is simply not true. Advisers are just trying to protect their territory by making it appear that it is just much too complicated for many of us to do ourselves. The irony is that many advisers do not spend a great deal of time on money management for their clients, opting instead to spend most of their working lives doing marketing to obtain more assets under management. While this strategy is clearly more profitable for the advisers, it does very little to enhance your net worth.

The concept of bond prices moving in the opposite direction to interest rates is not always understood even by the supposed experts. Many years ago, I worked with someone at a large financial institution who really had no idea how bond prices worked. This amazed me even more when the individual rose rapidly through the ranks to a senior management position in the organization. The individual was obviously very skilled at self- promoting to the upper levels of management. Once you realize that your adviser is not as financially savvy as you thought and is principally paid to be an asset gatherer rather than compensated by their investment recommendations, you will begin to see the light. Still I want to point out that there are many advisers who do have your best interests at heart, but they are often hard to find.

While investment management fees consistently remain high, investment returns continue to be quite volatile. Investors are clearly paying the price. One relatively easy solution is to minimize the fees you are paying by doing it yourself. This leaves much more in the till for you. Saving in excess of 1% annually compounded for many years adds up to a considerable sum of money that you will have for yourself to enjoy in your retirement and during your working lives.

Throughout my book, my objectives will continue to be reinforced to you. Improving your performance and consistency of your investment returns, lowering your fees and adequately diversifying your holdings to reduce risk will all become second nature to you once you have read and applied my comprehensive plan to take charge of your own investments.

Before improving your investment knowledge, my next chapter will ensure that all your debts are in order and your interest expenses are kept to a minimum.

OWN YOUR FINANCIAL FUTURE

TAKE CHARGE OF YOUR INVEST- MENTS

CHAPTER 1
MANAGE YOUR DEBTS AND START SAVING

How did we all get into this myriad of debt? Governments, corporations and personal debt levels are soaring. I will not go into an explanation of either the public or corporate debts in this chapter. My focus is exclusively on private debt – both the origins of it and how to deal with it effectively so it does not overwhelm your life. I also wish to share some ideas on establishing monthly savings plans away from your chequing account.

Many years ago, when my dad bought his first house, residential mortgages were relatively rare. At that time the availability of credit cards, lines of credit and credit in general was clearly not as it is today.

Banks and other financial institutions encouraged consumers to spend initially on homes through the introduction of residential mortgages and later on encouraged spending on other items by creating credit cards, car loans and lines of credit. We, the consumers, were guinea pigs following the bank's advice to spend, without being aware of the long-term consequences.

We need to realize that banks are in business to make money. They are not in business solely to help us. While they are at least partially responsible for getting us into debt, banks are not motivated to get us out of debt.

Even for those with little debt, banks encourage us to borrow to invest, which makes even more money for them. However, as I mention throughout this book, I never advise using someone else's money to try to make more. In a bear market this strategy normally ends in a financial disaster for the investor.

Banks use the terms "good" and "bad" debt. "Bad debt" refers to borrowing to spend on depreciable assets like a car, computer, clothing and furniture (unless it is antique.) On the other hand, "good debt" refers to borrowing to invest in assets that appreciate over time like a house or land for example. Banks frequently mention that this also includes investing in stocks. However, I personally do not classify this kind of debt as the good type.

Today many consumers have accumulated a massive amount of debt by investing in depreciable assets. Car loans and leases, credit cards and lines of credit are examples of this debt. In recent times, lines of credit, secured by the equity value in your home, have been used for almost any type of random spending. Differing from a traditional mortgage where your monthly payments are a blend of interest and capital repayment, lines of credit do not automatically involve any payment of principal. Most lines of credit have a variable rate of interest that can fluctuate depending on the Bank of Canada's interest rate policy. Many consumers only pay the minimum payment but never pay off any of their debt. This strategy is very dangerous, especially when interest rates eventually go back up again. If the banks really wanted to help you get out of debt, they would encourage you to repay more than the minimum payment. But they do not always do this.

RECOMMENDATIONS

Every month pay yourself first by saving a portion of your net pay and investing this sum into a separate no fee savings account away from your regular chequing account. This can be used for trips, presents and other items.

Invest another portion of your net pay into a balanced stock and bond low fee exchange traded fund. This payment can be part of your company's Group RRSP and if so, the sum will be taken off your paycheque with any tax break from the RRSP contribution being given immediately. If you are part of a government or private defined benefit pension plan, sign up as early as you can and start contributing.

Finally, if available, sign up to your company's stock ownership savings plan if your firm matches your contributions up to a certain limit.

Never spend more than you earn after tax. This is a recipe for disaster. In order to get out of debt, find out exactly what you are spending your money on. Do a full cash flow analysis on all your revenues and expenses on a monthly basis. Account for all the non-monthly annual, quarterly and other periodic expenses that affect your financial situation. Total these non-monthly expenses and divide by twelve to budget for them monthly. Add this additional monthly item to your regular monthly expenses. Every month when you receive your pay you should have some cash left over for these other expenses that you have not yet paid. Transfer this estimated additional monthly amount to a savings account. This ensures that you do not spend the money, but have the capital available to be used for those expenses when they become due. I am quite sure many consumers in debt who do not follow this strategy find themselves scrambling when a non-monthly expense comes due.

As you all know, credit card debt charges the highest rate of interest. It is a good idea to pay off this debt first. If you can consolidate all your debts into a low interest rate line of credit this would be of great help to you. Once you have completed a cash flow projection, you will be more aware of how much you have left every month. Even if it is a small amount, always try to pay more than your minimum monthly payment with the bank. In addition, if you receive an unanticipated bonus or any other payment, use some of this money to pay down your debts. It is normally a good idea to pay off your debts as fast as you can. However, as your residential mortgage debt already incorporates a capital repayment, concentrate on paying off your other debts first such as your credit card and line of credit.

Now that you are in control of your debts and spending habits, let's look at some fixed income investment options.

CHAPTER 2
FIXED INCOME INVESTING
WHAT ARE ALL YOUR OPTIONS?

The main objective of fixed income investments is both income generation and capital preservation. Please do not be intimidated by the number of options of fixed income securities I have listed below. Many of these you will never use, but it is helpful to understand the unique characteristics of each one.

It is important to take into account the liquidity of a fixed income security. Can you cash it in anytime without penalty?

Price volatility is determined by the combination of a security's average term to maturity and by the percentage of higher risk corporate bonds as a percentage of the total portfolio. My preference is investing in low fee bond ETFs that include both government and investment grade corporate securities.

The following securities are considered Fixed Income:
- Money Market Instruments – Canadian, US and global
- High Interest Savings Accounts – Canadian, US and global
- Regular Savings Accounts – Canadian, US and global
- Bank Guaranteed Investment Certificates (GICs) – Canadian and US
- Mortgages and Mortgage Funds and ETFs
- Canadian federal, provincial, municipal bonds and ETFs
- US federal, state, municipal bonds and ETFs
- Canadian and US investment grade bonds and ETFs
- Canadian High Yield Bonds and ETFs
- US High Yield Bonds and ETFs
- Private fixed income

This list is only a beginning, and could include many more types of securities. You might have noticed that preferred shares are not on this list. While these securities are income generating, they do not satisfy the capital preservation requirement. Preferred shares are really a type of equity and are highly volatile. I have come across many investors in recent years who have seen their market values of their preferred share holdings fall by as much as 40%. Rate reset preferreds, that make up a large percentage of most preferred funds and ETFs, go down when interest rates fall, a fact that is rarely understood properly by the vast majority of retail investors. I do not recommend preferred shares because of this high sensitivity to interest rates.

Normally the fixed income securities with the lowest level of risk are the lowest yielding ones. Consequently, money market instruments fit these criteria with very low yields. The funny thing about many money market funds is that they are not as risk free as one may think. Canada Deposit Insurance Corp (CDIC) provides capital guarantees up to $100,000 per financial institution. This guarantee includes savings and chequing accounts, GICs and US dollar bank accounts. However, this guarantee does not include mutual funds and ETFs, effectively excluding all money market funds.

Domestic and US Treasury bills offer a direct government guarantee but are only available in large amounts. This makes them a difficult choice for all but the large institutional and very high net worth investors.

Since high interest savings accounts are bank accounts they are included in the CDIC insurance. These accounts yield more than other short-term money market instruments and are normally available digitally online or in the branches.

Investing in bank GICs is another option for you, but these securities have several limitations that make me personally steer away from them. Non-cashable GICs cannot be cashed before maturity unless you are willing to forfeit all your interest. This lack of liquidity makes me avoid GICs under most circumstances. The only time I may consider investing in them is during a period when interest rates are rising and where bond prices are falling. GIC prices are not marked to market and always remain at your initial face value at purchase. I would avoid bank

GICs as a result of their lack of liquidity. As mentioned previously most bank GICs are covered by CDIC insurance, but not all.

In order to be absolutely sure which institutions are covered under CDIC insurance, you can go to their website at cdic.ca to verify this information.

Government of Canada bonds offer a direct guarantee for the payment of interest and principal at maturity by the Canadian government. Provincial and municipal bonds are guaranteed by their respective province and municipality respectively. US Treasury bonds are guaranteed by the US federal government. All bonds, including corporate ones, have returns consisting of both interest and capital gains.

Bond prices typically fluctuate in the opposite direction to interest rates. This differs from GICs that only have an interest component. When interest rates decline, bond prices rise as the fixed coupon yields makes them more attractive compared to current interest rates. The reverse is true when rates rise. Over the last many years interest rates have been steadily declining and this has greatly helped investment returns from bonds. At the current very low level of rates (historically) the probability of rates declining even further from here is relatively low. However, all the global central banks have indicated they will ensure that rates stay low well into 2022 to protect the economy from going back into another recession. Under this scenario bond returns will probably be considerably lower than over the last 5-10 years unless the world reverts back into a recessionary environment.

Investment grade corporate bonds provide higher returns than government bonds as a result of their credit risk. These bonds do not provide a guarantee from a government and are thus considered riskier. Despite these risks, many corporations with strong balance sheets and consistent and rising operating cash flows are not likely to go bankrupt or default on their debt payments. Bonds issued by most Canadian banks and utilities offer a much better yield than government bonds with only a slightly higher risk. The only caveat I would add at this point is that purchasing individual corporate bonds adds another level of risk over funds and ETFs in that these fixed income investments are much less diversified and consequently have a higher risk. If you choose to purchase individual corporate bonds over funds and ETFs, I caution you to be very careful about the percentage invested in any single bond.

Investing in high yield bonds and ETFs involves more credit risk than investment grade ones. This type of security involves investing in poorer credits where the probability of default is much higher. Consequently, I only recommend high yield bond ETFs rather than individual issues as the risk of default of one issue is minimized by the diversity of the holdings.

Length of term is also an important factor in fixed income investing. The longer the term, the more price volatility. Taking into account the low level of interest rates at this time, I advise investing in shorter term bond ETFs as the risk is much lower.

My experience working in the investment industry for my entire career has led me to the following recommendations. The retail investor ends up paying higher embedded commissions when transacting in smaller positions of individual bonds. This is not readily transparent. While a stock's commission is clearly highlighted, this is not the case with bonds. The commission is hidden in the price you pay and consequently many retail investors end up getting hurt as a result. Purchasing and selling quantities of bonds, up to $500,000 for each purchase or sale, is considered a very small transaction for institutional investors. The poor retail investor ends up with lower yields as a result of these liquidity issues. The main way to avoid this is to only purchase new issues when they become available and to hold them until maturity. You can do this with relatively smaller quantities. However, this is not without its own problems as any one issue may not satisfy your specific preference of investing in one maturity. The other negative is a lack of diversification.

CONCLUSION

Investing in bonds involves taking many factors into consideration including liquidity, income generation, capital preservation, credit risk, price volatility, average term and the level and direction of interest rates. For the lack of liquidity characteristics, I do not like investing in GICs. I also do not like investing in individual bonds under most circumstances due to their higher embedded commissions for smaller quantities transacted.

My advice is to purchase a low fee Bond ETF that includes both government and investment grade corporate issues. Do not look at past performance as any indication of future results when investing in bonds. Pay close attention to the amount of credit risk and the average term to maturity to minimize the price volatility. When purchasing a bond ETF, it is important to look at the fund's average weighted yield to maturity and not to simply look at the purchase yield. Private fixed income securities offer a higher yield than traditional bonds but they are much less liquid and only available to very high net worth clients.

Now that you are more aware of your fixed income options, we can begin the process of opening up a discount brokerage account.

CHAPTER 3
HOW TO OPEN AN ACCOUNT AND START TRADING STOCKS AND ETFS

In this chapter you will learn how to open up a discount brokerage account and how to trade individual securities and ETFs. ETFs are bought and sold on the stock exchange only. You may want to open up several different types of accounts and hold different securities in each one in order to maximize any tax benefits. Additionally, I will explain how to transact and summarize the difference between the bid and ask prices when you get to the trading platform. Being able to invest in individual securities and ETFs will provide you with a feeling of power, knowing you are now in full control over your own financial affairs. You will be able to take advantage of market opportunities when they present themselves and relish in the fact that you no longer need to rely on someone else for advice. This is powerful and good for the psyche. However, you still must learn how to choose the securities for your portfolio and to manage it effectively for the rest of your life.

For those of you who invest regularly for your own accounts, the following chapter may seem quite elementary. However, I know that many of you have never invested in an individual security and have no idea how to proceed if so desired. Some of you have the good fortune of having a defined benefit pension plan through your employment. In the past these plans were offered to employees working for both corporations and federal, provincial and municipal governments. Today the high cost of maintaining and administering such plans combined with the drawback of honouring the liabilities incurred have largely relegated the availability of pension plans to governments and some large financial institutions. Group RRSPs, considered a cheaper alternative to defined benefit pension plans, are a more cost- efficient option for employers to help their employees with their retirement planning.

So let's begin. The first thing you want to do is determine which discount broker you want to deal with. Most banks have discount broker divisions. As well, you may choose an independent firm like Questrade. For convenience purposes, you may want to investigate if your bank offers discount brokerage services. Then, if you need some money in your bank account or vice versa, it is very easy to transfer between your bank account and your discount brokerage account, and you can usually do this the same day. If you decide to deal with a different company from your bank, it is still relatively easy to transfer monies but it normally can take several days.

Personally, I set up discount broker accounts at the same bank I deal with and this has worked out very well. There are various websites online that rank domestic discount brokers by various criteria. You may want to review these sites to ensure you are getting exactly what you want. Every discount broker offers something unique from the others, so it is entirely up to you to choose the one that meets your needs. Large firms tend to have a fair amount of investment research on their sites. That can be helpful to you in your security selection. However, some of you may subscribe to a service that already provides the research you need and you may not need this information. In this case a smaller discount broker with lower commission rates per transaction may be a better alternative.

Once you settle on a discount broker, you can determine both the number and type of accounts you plan to open. If you are married, you will want to open a joint non-registered account in addition to a non registered one in your name only. If one of you prefers making the investment decisions, you can give your trading authority to the other to trade on all your accounts, not just the joint one. If this makes you uncomfortable in any way, you can revoke this discretion anytime. Or you can permit your authorization for your personal accounts only with joint authorization for your joint account.

While these details appear to be only subtle differences, they are clearly not, especially in the case of a marriage breakdown.

Opening a joint or individual margin account is useful if you plan on borrowing to invest. While I do not advise borrowing for any type of investors, novice or sophisticated, setting up a margin account at the onset just gives you some flexibility. In addition to your joint account, you may also want to open an individual non-registered account. You will also both need to open individual RRSP and Registered Retirement Income Accounts (RRIF's) if applicable. Then to complete your investment holdings you will both need to open Tax-Free Savings accounts (TFSAs.). The main difference between an RRSP and a TFSA is that the former's contributions are tax deductible while contributions to a TFSA are not. TFSA's have the advantage of never being taxed either when the monies are in the plan or withdrawn. On the other hand, RRSPs are taxable when withdrawn with two exceptions: withdrawals from a RRSP to either purchase your first home or to enhance your education are not taxed. However, they must be repaid back into the plans over a fifteen year period for the Home Buyer's Plan and over 10 years for the Lifelong Learning Plan.

The other major difference between these two accounts is that US withholding taxes for US dividends are payable in a TFSA, but not in a registered account. You will still be hit with US withholding taxes in a non-registered account, but you will receive a tax credit that can reduce your Canadian taxes payable. To qualify for this, you must fill out a W-8Ben tax form to prove you are a Canadian resident and that you only pay a 15% US withholding tax on US dividends, not the 30% for your non-registered accounts.

I also recommend setting up joint and/or individual US dollar accounts to hold your US investments. By doing this you will make sure that any US dividend income is kept in US dollars and not automatically converted into Canadian dollars. In addition, opening up a separate US RRSP and/or RRIF avoids any US withholding taxes on US dividends.

The trading platform of all discount broker firms may initially seem confusing to you if you have never traded a stock before. You will see a trading table that asks you for the name of the security, the number of shares you want to buy or sell and if you are purchasing or selling the security. You will need to be certain of the stock's trading symbol and exchange where it trades and where you want to transact. You will also notice a bunch of choices for the type of orders. I will not get into all the types at this time but will highlight the ones I use regularly to trade.

On your discount brokerage website, you can read about the many types of trading orders that are available to simplify your trading activities. It is essential to completely understand them before using them. The rationale for having so many types of orders is to help you place your orders and transact efficiently during your working day when you may not be able to check up on your transactions on an hourly basis. If you are working full time and you don't want your boss to monitor all your activities online, I would restrict going onto your discount brokerage site to three times daily – the first one just before the markets open at 9:30 am Eastern Standard Time, during your lunch and finally just before the market closes at 4pm.

The stock market is an auction and this can be clearly seen when transacting in a security. When you are purchasing a stock, you are competing with all the other buyers. The bid price you see at the time you place your trade represents the highest price any current buyer is willing to pay for at least one board lot representing 100 shares. The same is true for all the sellers. You are all competing to sell your shares.

The offering price you see on your screen represents the lowest price that any seller is willing to sell at least one board lot. A market order means that you will purchase the security at the lowest offering price at the time of placing the order. Please keep in mind that a market order does not request a specific price, so it may end up being higher than you thought originally when purchasing or lower when selling. A market sell order means that you are willing to sell your shares at the highest price a bidder is willing to pay for them.

Another type of order is called a limit order. In this case you set a maximum limit price when buying and minimum selling price when selling. I use this type of order normally. It is important to keep in mind that you may never transact if your bid limit price is lower than the current highest bid price and if your minimum offering price is higher than the lowest offering price on the market at that time. If you choose to use a limit order, you will need to check your order status frequently to ensure that your limit price remains competitive.

A stop loss order is another type and there are two versions – a market and limit stop loss. For a stop loss order, you want to continue holding the stock, but do not want it to drop sharply without having an opportunity to sell at a higher price. A stop loss with a market order means that if the stock drops below a certain level that you assign, the shares are subsequently sold at the best market price bid at that time. Alternatively, a stop loss with a limit is the same as the former except that you are not willing to sell your shares at any price. You set a limit price that you are comfortable with. In the latter case you may not end up selling if the price drops too quickly.

The difference between the bid and the offer is called the spread. For illiquid securities the spread can be quite wide. When you are placing your order you will see the current bid and offering price plus some other numbers beside both the bid and asking price. These other numbers refer to the number of board lots of shares that are bid at the current bid price and the corresponding number of board lots for sale at the offering price. A board lot refers to 100 shares for most companies, so if you see a number 1 beside the bid it refers to 100 shares. You can still transact with less than a board lot number of shares but your transaction price will be somewhat negatively affected. Do not let that discourage you, as many US companies in particular trade at very high price valuations. You can purchase an odd lot that represents less than the board lot of 100 shares any time you want. I personally do it regularly for high priced securities where I need to ensure I properly diversify across securities and industries and not to have too much invested in one security. Buying odd lots enables you to do this.

When you see the number of board lots on the bid side far exceeding the number on the offering side, this usually indicates strong demand for the security. Alternatively, when you see the reverse it indicates selling pressure.

CONCLUSION

This chapter covered the logistics of opening up investment accounts with a discount broker and learning how to trade individual stocks and ETFs in these accounts. Gaining the knowledge to trade individual stocks and ETFs will give you a sense of power and control. Understanding the logistics of doing this is not as difficult as it sounds. Once you get used to it you will really start to enjoy it. But remember to always do your research to make sure you have all the facts before making a transaction.

Now that you are more familiar with opening up discount broker accounts and trading on your own, the next chapter will summarize how to switch your high cost mutual funds into Exchange Traded Funds while keeping redemption fees as low as possible.

CHAPTER 4

HOW TO SWITCH YOUR
MUTUAL FUNDS INTO ETFS

Owning high cost mutual funds will not provide you with the investment returns you will need to retire comfortably and live the life you want. Many of you still own lots of mutual funds but are unsure how to switch them into a more cost efficient alternative. What are the logistics to make the switch while simultaneously ensuring that all redemption fees are kept to a minimum?

In this chapter I will provide you with a step by step approach to liquidate your funds and switch them into a much lower cost alternative of ETFs. I have recommended this approach to many investors. Some have taken my advice, while others have gone back to their current advisers asking them what to do. Why would your adviser suggest anything but staying with them as this is the best monetary option for them?

If you can save thousands of dollars by following my advice, this saving will end up materially enhancing your net worth. Taking into account that most ETFs are managed by the same people as the ones who manage your mutual funds, you may begin to wake up and see the light. Switching around your investments into much lower fee ETFs is a no brainer in my opinion, especially when the ETFs have largely the identical risk parameters as your mutual funds. I would never advise you to sell your mutual funds before obtaining the details of the deferred sales charges(DSC's) remaining on your funds held. This could result in a hefty 5.5% deferred sales charge (DSC) on your capital invested if you are too hasty in your selling of your mutual funds.

My goal in writing this book is only to help and encourage you to save the high fees you are currently paying by switching to a more cost efficient alternative. I have no other hidden agenda. A couple who I advised several years ago to make the switch out of mutual funds into ETFs said:

When we found out about Peter McMurtry's broad financial expertise and experience, we asked our former neighbor to help us transition our portfolio from mutual funds into exchange traded funds (ETFs) for the sole purpose of reducing ongoing management fees. We had looked into this on several earlier occasions, but the task seemed too daunting to tackle ourselves.

Peter started with quickly and efficiently reviewing our existing portfolio to ensure that any future transition into ETFs would not incur unexpected deferred sales charges or unrealized capital gains, something we would never have thought about doing ourselves. After this was done, Peter advised and coached us very effectively with the creation of our ETF portfolio and the selection of a reputable self-service broker.

Peter then guided us through the process of transferring our existing portfolio to the selected brokerage and met with us on more than one occasion to teach us the ins-and-outs of the brokerage websites and helped us make the initial ETF purchases on-line. Although we knew that the transition to the EFT portfolio would result in significant long- term savings for us, we would never have completed this process without Peter's help and encouragement.

As the result of the changes made with Peter's invaluable help, we were able to minimize our ongoing management fees as well as eliminating the asset mix fee that our former advisor charged. This resulted in a substantial annual savings in the range of 1.5-2.5% of our overall capital invested. The exchange traded funds purchased all had at least similar (or better) return and risk characteristics than our mutual funds had.

Peter greatly helped us ensure that our retirement savings would last considerably longer and that our overall net worth was materially enhanced. And, as icing on the cake, he did this with a smile and patience. We very much appreciate Peter's work and the results.

Putting blind faith in your adviser to always do what is in your best interest is a foolish idea. Regardless if your adviser is a close friend or even a family member, their bosses force them to act in the interest of the corporation where they work. You, as one of their clients, are simply there to inflate the adviser's assets under management and the sooner you realize this, the better.

As many of you have discovered, deferred sales charges on mutual funds still apply after six years of ownership for many fund companies. In my opinion this is a recipe for disaster to invest in a security where very high liquidation fees are charged for many years. Where is the accountability for poor performance? These fund companies routinely take advantage of clients and profit from them whether or not the investment performance is good or bad.

I can only advise what is best for you. I cannot force you into something you do not want. However, my job is to ensure that you are looking after your personal interests first and not simply staying with your current provider for fear of hurting their feelings. It is important to take charge and be pro-active with your financial decisions before it is too late.

Steps to Follow

Before you start liquidating your mutual funds, determine what DSC fees remain and what the annual management fees of your current funds are. This latter fee is provided to you in percentage terms and is called the MER, management expense ratio. Many mutual funds have both DSCs and high ongoing management fees, making the decision to switch even easier. There are no DSC fees on ETFs and they differ from mutual funds in that they trade on the stock exchange like a stock. You will need to pay a small commission to transact. For some online discount brokers the commission to purchase and sell ETFs is waived. The ongoing MER fee information for both mutual funds and ETFs is available online. Simply go directly to the fund company's website and click fund facts for each fund in question.

I advise not asking your current adviser to gather this information for you. If you do this, they will do everything in their power to keep you as clients, even though this may not be what is best financially for you.

You will need to call the head office of all the mutual fund companies you own and request this information from the client services department. Keep your statements handy when you call as the mutual fund will need the details of the funds you hold. The employees in the client services area are there to help get the information requested in a timely fashion and you should not feel intimidated in any way. Ask the following questions to each mutual fund company:

1. What is the dollar value and number of units of the DSCs remaining for each mutual fund held?

2. What are the actual number of fee free units available now that you can sell any time without incurring any sales charges?

3. What are the expiry dates of the DSC fees for every fund held?

As soon as you have determined the number of fee free units, you can place the order to sell these units without any worries about sales charges. The next thing you will do is immediately cease all monthly, quarterly or annual contributions into the mutual funds you currently hold. This step ensures that you will minimize any future sales charges that can be charged up to seven years after purchase.

Once your fee free units are sold, you can ask the head office of the mutual fund company what remaining deferred sales charges there are and when they expire. Every year you will need to call the mutual fund company to ask them the same list of questions and this must be done until all of your load funds have been liquidated. It is your responsibility to instruct the mutual fund companies annually to sell all your fee free units.

After you complete the verification of fees, you may still want to switch your remaining DSC load funds into ETFs. Before you decide on this option, compare the annual management fees (MER's) for both your current mutual funds and for comparable ETFs that you are considering purchasing. Calculate the number of years for you to break even. For example, if the difference in annual fees (MER's) is 1.25% and you have $300,000 invested, this works out to an annual savings of $3,750 by making the switch into the lower cost ETF. Now compare the DSC fee remaining on your mutual fund held with the annual cost saving of $3,750. In this specific case, if the DSC fee remaining is $3,750 then you will break even in one year by making the switch. You may want to work out a break even compromise that works for you. After making all these calculations, you may decide to only liquidate the 10% fee free units annually or you may decide to sell all your funds now and incur a redemption fee that will be recoverable shortly by investing in much lower fee ETFs.

CONCLUSION

Once you have seen the light and want to take the management of your own capital into your hands, making this switch out of high fee mutual funds into ETFs will seem very logical to you. Your net worth is certainly going to be enhanced with lower ongoing fees. All you need to do is to ensure you verify all your remaining DSC fees first and then to liquidate your fee free units for every one of your mutual funds. You may even decide to liquidate all your funds, pay the redemption fees and invest in much lower fee ETFs if the period to recoup your sales charges is not too long. It is totally up to you. You are finally in the driver's seat.

Now that I have shown you how to liquidate your mutual funds without incurring large redemption fees, you are about to see the major differences between owning mutual and exchange traded funds and individual stocks and bonds.

CHAPTER 5
WHAT ARE THE BEST
INVESTMENT OPTIONS?

Which is best – a portfolio of Mutual Funds, Exchange Traded Funds or Individual Stocks and Bonds? As retail investors, we all want to know the best way to invest in order to earn solid investment returns and attractive dividend yields. Many of us really do not care if our portfolios consist of mutual or exchange traded funds (ETFs), individual stocks and bonds or a combination of the above. However, we are learning very quickly that ongoing management and deferred sales charges can significantly eat into our returns, leaving much less for us in our retirement years. Most of us do not feel that our financial advisers deserve to take a larger slice of our capital than we earn ourselves.

In this chapter I will demonstrate that owning individual securities as opposed to mutual or exchange traded funds is really not as scary as many of you have been led to believe. In fact, buying and holding high quality stocks can lower your fees and give you much more control over your financial destiny.

Investing in high cost mutual funds is gradually being replaced with exchange traded funds due to the much lower fees. When Exchange Traded Funds (ETFs) were first introduced they compared very favourably to mutual funds. Much lower management fees, no deferred sales charges, better performance, more strategic tax efficiency are factors that investors need to know to make the switch out of mutual funds into ETFs. Another major difference between mutual funds and ETFs is that the latter are bought and sold on the stock exchange like a stock, while mutual fund transactions can only be executed through the fund company. In the previous chapter I highlighted the steps to follow to make the transition out of mutual funds into ETFs. It is important to follow all the steps in sequence to ensure that no deferred sales charges are applied that eat into your capital.

Today there are so many types of ETFs and mutual funds that many investors really do not understand what they are invested in and how much risk these investments incorporate.

The basic principle of mutual funds and ETFs is risk reduction through diversification. The influx of sector and active ETFs both on the long and short side of the market has materially added a level of risk that was not the case for passive index ETFs of the overall major market indices. Equity sector ETFs invest in any of the eleven sub-sectors of the market including technology, financials, utilities, healthcare, materials and energy. Investing in only one or a few of these groups and excluding the others exposes your investments to industry risk that is quite different than the overall market risk.

Many of you have probably heard the term active vs passive investing. Passive index investing refers to investing in an index of the overall market that includes exposure to all eleven sectors. The major benefit of this type of investment is that your equity investments are well diversified. The major negative is that in a bear market your investments will decline as much as the market as there is nowhere to hide. Active investment strategies refer to targeted investments that differ from the overall market to take advantage of market opportunities in specific sectors and companies with a unique advantage. This approach gives the investor the opportunity to perform better than the overall market, but also exposes the portfolio to unique non-market risk. Sector investing is one form of active investing.

The graph below compares an investment in an ETF called Financial 15 Split Corp. (FFN) with the share price performance of Royal Bank. According to the website, this security invests in "a high quality portfolio of Canadian and US financial services companies". Taking into consideration its 45.6% collapse in share price over the last three years ending January 22, 2021, I discovered the fund is using leverage to borrow more capital to invest in the same underlying financial securities. Leverage only works to the investor's benefit when the markets are rising and has a magnified negative effect in a falling equity market. On a total return basis (dividend plus capital gain or loss) FFN showed a negative annualized return over the same three- year period of 8.65%, far worse than RBC's positive

3.94% respectively. These differences are quite dramatic and are largely a result of the amount of leverage used. Any investors owing this security thinking it was low risk were clearly astonished by the results.

FFN vs Royal Bank

New ETFs are being created every day that supposedly satisfy client's needs for equity participation in sectors of the market such as biotech, cannabis, bitcoin, country-specific emerging markets and cyber-security. This endless list is expanding continuously.

Despite the benefits of these trends, the traditional advantage of risk reduction from market diversification is being overshadowed by the sharp increase in unique risk. This risk is not being adequately conveyed to retail investors by the creators of ETFs and mutual funds who are principally driven by increasing their revenues at the expense of everything else.

Well-informed investors, with individual securities, can foresee a market correction, and can take risk off the table by adding more cash and reducing their equity exposure in more volatile sectors. Stock picking and industry selection become even more important in a falling market.

Individual stock investing has unfairly received a bad rap for being too risky for many investors. However stock investing can produce superior returns with lower risk than many ETFs and mutual funds. This is done by being sufficiently diversified across all eleven equity sectors, combined with spreading the risk by investing in both value, growth, small, large cap and international companies. In addition raising cash and reducing exposure to more volatile stocks and equity sectors is a good strategy in a recession.

Furthermore, analyzing individual companies is much easier than attempting to do research on ETFs or mutual funds. Lack of transparency, limited disclosure of material factors and a short historical track record make ETF or mutual fund investing much riskier than a disciplined investment of individual stocks. Basic fundamental stock analysis is just not possible with ETFs and mutual funds. In most cases the security regulators only require the top ten holdings and this is simply not sufficient to accurately determine the level of risk assumed. As well, the holdings can change frequently and this makes the investment analysis even more difficult.

Good fundamental stock selection on individual companies produces a factor called alpha that is the unique advantage that one company has over its peers. Alpha is defined as the excess returns created by investing in companies that beat their benchmark indices. This is the factor that the best money managers such as Peter Lynch, John Templeton and Warren Buffet have used to create their superior long-term performance. An investment in an ETF or mutual fund largely ignores or greatly waters down the benefits of alpha, although there are some active ETFs and funds with this goal in mind. Please review the attached graph below on Shopify, Canada's high tech darling. On a cumulative basis over the last three years, the shares are up a staggering 923%, while the TSX Capped Composite ETF is up only 9.4% on a total return basis. Shopify does not pay a dividend. Owning a diversified exchange traded fund that includes Shopify clearly would not have produced equivalent returns compared to owing the latter company directly.

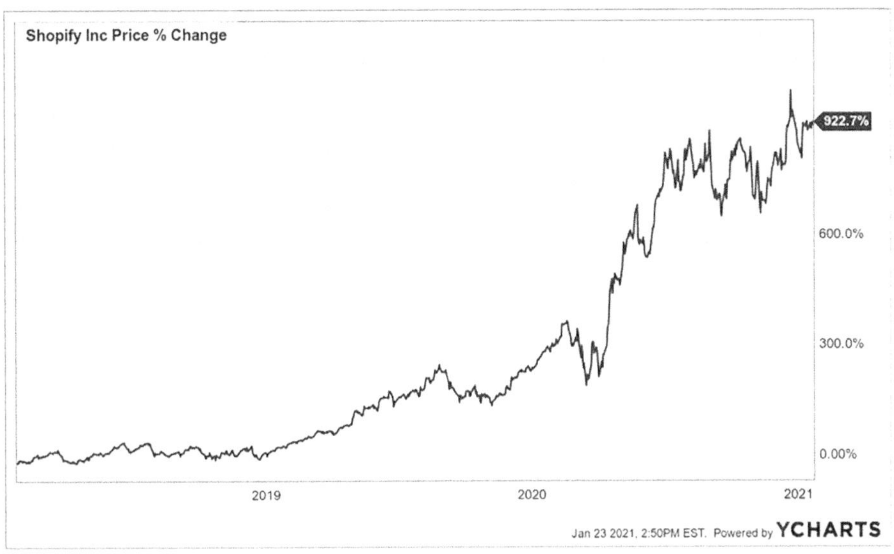

Shopify - price % change

Frequently during my thirty years in this money management business, I have heard many retail client advisers belittle the benefits of stock picking. Clients deserve better. The decision to invest in an ETF or mutual fund that may hold a small investment in a superior stock will almost always water down the benefits of investing directly in that stock. Retail clients may think they are getting superior stock picking from their adviser, but this is clearly not always the case.

CONCLUSION

Many retail investors are branching away from their investment advisers in order to improve their performance, lower their fees and lower their risk. I recommend that every investor spend more time understanding exactly what they are invested in, even if they have limited financial knowledge. The first step for you is to gradually switch your investments out of high cost mutual funds into a combination of individual securities and some ETFs. Care must be taken to minimize or avoid completely if possible, any remaining deferred sales charges on your mutual funds.

Now that you have been shown the different investment options available, you are about to learn how to set up and manage the asset mix of your investments.

CHAPTER 6
HOW TO DETERMINE
AN APPROPRIATE ASSET MIX

The single most important factor in your long- term investment performance is the asset mix of your holdings. It is more important than either your stock or equity sector selection. Always keep in mind that stocks tend to go up around 80% of the time. However, when they start declining you really do not want to be fully invested in them, nor do you want to be invested with borrowed funds. During the depression of 1929 where many investors were on margin, borrowing large sums of money with the stocks as collateral, there were many stories of people jumping off buildings and bridges to avoid the humiliation of bankruptcy and financial ruin.

When I first got into this business, an older work colleague told me how he had made a lot of money in the stock market by borrowing heavily. He went on a fancy vacation with his wife and family before he had sold his stocks. During his vacation the markets collapsed and he not only lost all his own capital, but had an enormous debt to pay back to the broker. He chose not to file for bankruptcy as he was a proud man. It took him over twenty years to pay the money back.

There are two types of asset mix strategies that financial companies use with their clients. These types of asset allocation strategies are referred to as "tactical" or "strategic". Strategic allocation is your long-term asset allocation based on your individual needs and objectives. Factors such as income needs, risk tolerance, time horizon and tax considerations are taken into account in the determination of your asset mix. The short-term outlook for the security markets are not really taken into consideration in this asset mix calculation. Normally once or twice a year the financial adviser rebalances your current asset mix back to the long-term percentages that you established at the beginning. During the year markets can fluctuate greatly and these short-term movements can make any portfolio out of alignment with their long-term percentage weights.

It is important to note that these rebalancing measures are reactionary and are not based on the market's outlook. They are simply done to get the portfolio back to its long-term objective and are largely robotic changes that can be done by a computer. On the other hand, tactical asset allocation strategies are based on the current outlook for security markets and are considered pro-active in nature. Both strategies have strengths and weaknesses. Robotically selling stocks in the strategic asset mix approach after they have run up in value is not always a bad strategy to follow. Alternatively, tactical asset mix strategies that can predict an upcoming bear market can save you a lot of money by being in cash in the middle of a market meltdown.

Personally, I use a combination of both strategies where I have a percentage range of the weights for all three asset classes – namely Cash, Bonds and Stocks, instead of a fixed percentage. This gives me a lot of flexibility to increase or decease my weight in stocks and the other asset classes based on the immediate outlook for the markets. An example would be an equity percentage range from 40-60%. This wide range gives the investor a lot of flexibility to increase or decrease the stock exposure depending on the market outlook.

While equity markets go up most of the time, the real strengths of the best money managers become more clearly evident in a bear market where they use active asset mix strategies to minimize portfolio volatility. Reducing equity holdings, raising cash and minimizing equity sector weights in cyclical industries are all risk reducing strategies that need to be pursued in a bear market. There is a fair amount of debate about these market timing strategies. Many financial institutions prefer not to even attempt to sell equities, preferring only to focus on the long term. Regardless of their rhetoric, many large pension funds regularly use active asset mix policies to either reduce or increase portfolio volatility at opportune times. In my opinion, active asset mix strategies significantly add value, but they require a fair amount of market discipline and analysis to be carried out effectively. Please note that I have purposely excluded short selling as a risk reducing strategy as this involves margin calls when markets go up.

We all know the enormous popularity of index funds and ETFs in recent years. Many advisers do not even focus on individual securities, categorizing them as much too risky compared to a more diversified fund or ETF. I believe that every one of you can create your own personalized fund that is much more attuned to your specific objectives. By taking an active approach to your investments, you can greatly reduce your level of portfolio risk in a bear market and consequently minimize your anxiety.

One retired gentleman I met remained fully invested during most bull and bear markets. My wife clearly pointed out to me the foolishness of his approach. His reasoning behind being totally invested in stocks in a bear market is that he has no external corporate or government pension and relies on income generated from his investments and from Canada Pension Plan and Old Age Security. During the last recession of 2007-2008, he was fully invested in stocks. It took him over seven years to break even on the market value of his holdings and, incredibly, he seemed quite proud of this fact. In a recession many companies cut their dividends, so you really cannot rely on them to maintain them. Secondly, if you see a massive 30-40% decline in your investments, there is a real possibility of getting so stressed out that you may have a heart attack. Earning a 4-5% dividend on a stock where its share price ends up falling by 40% is not a good strategy for me. I don't need to be a mathematician to see that the total return from this investment was a negative 35%.

It is important to review the economic outlook every month to ensure that a recession is not imminent. One good place to start is the government's current monetary and fiscal policy. I tend to focus on the US economic numbers rather than our domestic numbers, as both the size of their economy and proximity to us make what happens in the US of paramount importance.

Fiscal policy refers to government spending, with more stimulus normally a good indicator for future growth. I also review the US Federal Reserve's position on interest rates, economic growth and the outlook for inflation. Historically, when the US Central Bank has an accommodative monetary policy, they keep interest rates as low as possible and increase the money supply as fast as possible. This is exactly what they are doing right now. This is reinforced by the Federal

Reserve's ongoing Quantitative Easing Program, which involves the purchase of longer term US Treasury bonds to keep interest rates low. However, if inflation should suddenly sharply accelerate later this year or next, the Central Bank may be forced to reverse their current accommodative monetary policy by raising rates.

The US Treasury 10-year minus 2-year yield curve is a useful indicator to measure the probability of an upcoming recession. Historically the spread between the 10- and 2-year yields turns negative approximately six months before an economic downturn. Currently the spread in early February 2021, is positive and rising from year end.

Next I review the US investment grade Corporate Bond spread over 10-year US Treasury bonds. Historically in past recessions, the corporate bond spread widens sharply indicating that large pension funds have lost confidence in corporate bonds from staying out of financial problems. During a strong economy confidence picks up and large institutional money managers purchase corporate bonds with the yield advantage over US Treasuries. This results in corporate bond spreads narrowing, as is the case right now. During the last recession of 2007-2008, Baa rated corporate bond spreads over US Treasuries reached levels in excess of 6% with high yield corporate bond spreads climbing in excess of 11%. As of the end of January Baa rated corporate bond spreads were at 2.17% with US high yield under 4%.

CONCLUSION

Hopefully I have instilled in you a desire to actively manage your asset mix to minimize portfolio volatility. Replacing your equity index funds with individual securities is a good place to start this process. Combining both your strategic long-term objectives with a current assessment of the security market outlook will greatly help you improve the consistency of your investment returns.

This involves making a short term tactical asset mix call that addresses the probability of an upcoming economic recession. Keeping track that both government monetary and fiscal policies remain expansionary will be an important task to ensure that economic growth remains in an uptrend. If the economic indicators are showing some red flags, then raising some cash, increasing your fixed income weight, reducing your equity exposure and rotating into more defensive stocks are strategies to minimize portfolio volatility.

Now that you are more comfortable with asset mix strategies, you are about to see how to set up and manage an investment portfolio.

HOW TO SET UP AND MANAGE AN INVESTMENT PORTFOLIO

A portfolio is not simply a bunch of stocks and bonds you have bought randomly without any thought of how each security relates to the others. The construction of a portfolio is instrumental in the returns you will receive and the volatility or risk of these returns. Before you set up a portfolio, it is important to determine its overall objective as well as any investment constraints that you may have. Your investment time horizon, income needs and level of risk you are comfortable assuming are all important factors to take into account. Tax matters also play a role in portfolio construction, especially in relation to what type of account holds what security. In terms of portfolio size, I would try to accumulate at least $10,000 before purchasing individual stocks. In the interim, you can invest in a low-cost balanced ETF.

Categorize every security you purchase into different asset classes such as Cash and equivalents, Fixed Income, Preferred shares and Common shares. Fixed income consists of bank GICs, government bonds, investment grade and high yield corporate bonds. Common equities include Canadian, US and international equities.

Consolidated Asset Mix

For the many of you who already own stocks and have established a portfolio, I want to ensure that you will learn to properly set up and manage an investment portfolio. My advice for every investor, both the Do It Yourself and those with an adviser, is to add up the market values of all your investments from every account you have and to create a consolidated asset mix. For US and foreign currency holdings, I recommend taking the Canadian dollar equivalent of every security in the determination of the consolidated asset mix. For any equity and fixed income investments in mutual funds and ETFs, it is important to review the asset mix, equity sector weights, the percentage exposure of both corporate and government bonds in the overall mix, in addition to the fixed income's average term to maturity. All these factors determine how much risk your portfolio has. The level of risk you take is important to the absolute returns you will be receiving. Generally speaking, the lower the portfolio risk the more consistent your investment returns will be.

Try to establish a personalized asset mix that incorporates both minimum and maximum percentage weights for every asset class. This involves combining your long-term goals with the current market outlook and gives you some flexibility to alter your asset mix when market opportunities present themselves. These are active asset mix strategies. Many financial institutions frown on market timing strategies, but in reality they are very effective in both minimizing your overall portfolio risk in a bear market and increasing your level of risk when valuations become attractive, especially during the initial stages of a new bull market.

Fixed Income Investments

Many investors do not worry much about the risk they are taking with their fixed income investments. This is not wise.

Owning a fixed income mutual fund or ETF does not automatically reduce your overall risk through diversification. It is important to dissect all the investments of each fund or ETF held to determine the following factors:

- Investment Grade of fixed income holdings – percentage in investment grade, high yield corporates and government bonds
- Average term and duration of your fixed income investments
- Yield to Maturity is much more important than simply looking at average yield

For individual corporate bonds, it is important to see what the percentage weight is for each corporate issuer, with a higher percentage indicating more risk.

Equity Sector Weights

The equity component of your portfolio is divided into eleven individual and unique sectors that perform very differently from each other. You will find the sectors and their corresponding weights on the website: *https://www.spglobal.com* for both the TSX Composite Index in Canada and the S&P 500 index in the US.

Once you are on the website, click indices and search for specific country indices that I mentioned above. The eleven sectors are as follows: Financials, Energy, Materials, Industrials, Consumer Discretionary, Communication Services, Consumer Staples, Technology, Utilities, Real Estate and Healthcare. These index weights are updated every month.

Once I have these percentages, I pro-rate each country - namely Canada and the US - to create a North American equity sector benchmark weight. Currently I am using a 50-50% split but this can be adjusted anytime depending on the economic and currency outlook for each country. Lastly I determine my own unique equity sector weight based on both the benchmark weights and the economic outlook for each sector. The cyclical sector weights can be adjusted more frequently as a result of an assessment on the strength of an economic recovery and the probability of going into another recession. Cyclical groups include Financials, Energy, Materials and Industrials. Real Estate has become more cyclical as a result of the recent pandemic and its effect on monthly rents.

If you are having difficulty choosing the weight of each sector, I recommend starting with the benchmark weights on the website: https://www.spglobal.com/ spdji/en/indices/equity/sp-500/#overview and then calculate a North American benchmark weight. When you become comfortable you can adjust both the North American percentages and the actual sector weight based on your outlook.

Individual Stock Selection

Once you have established your asset mix percentage range weights and your equity sector exposure, you can begin the process of stock selection.

In terms of choosing individual stocks, begin with each equity sector and do some investment analysis on the major companies in each group. Please refer to my chapter on stock investment analysis to assist you in this process. Try to have stock exposure to every major group to minimize portfolio volatility. Make sure that you limit your purchases to a maximum limit of 3-5% in any one stock as a percentage of all your stocks held. Over time, if your stock selection is good, the weight in any one stock could reach 10% in a strong market. Once a year it is always a good idea to take some profits in your winners by reducing their weights somewhat if they get close to 10%. This does not mean selling your entire holding, but only trimming back to keep the percentage weights below a threshold of around 10% of all stocks.

The financial sector is the largest sector in Canada by percentage weight and is one of the top five in the US market. This group includes traditional banks, investment banks, insurance companies and large mutual fund and ETF companies. Domestic companies include Royal and TD Bank, Intact Financial and Sun Life. US companies include JP Morgan, Bank of America, Morgan Stanley, T. Rowe Price and Allstate. Never simply add a company to your portfolio because you are familiar with it. You still need to complete your investment research.

After you select a few companies in each country in every sector, go to the next one and do the same process. Once you have gone through all eleven sectors you will probably end up with 40-45 names plus some fixed income ETFs and some global ones as well. Treat this as your personalized mutual fund with much lower costs and much better aligned to your specific situation.

Many of you will want to ensure your picks produce a certain level of dividend income. This is easy to do with dividend yields being readily available.

Correlation of investment returns of one company relative to the overall market

Before you decide to add BCE to your portfolio when you already have Telus and Rogers, it is important to determine a stock's correlation with the market.

A stock's correlation coefficient can range from -1 to +1. If a stock has a correlation coefficient of -1, it means that if the market goes up by 20%, the stock will go down by the same percentage. If a stock has a +1 correlation with the overall market, the stock will fall by the same percentage as the market in a downturn.

The objective for investors is to own some stocks with positive correlations to the market and some stocks with negative correlations so that they all balance out to zero. In no way does this imply that your absolute price returns will be zero. It is only another guide to help you control the level of portfolio risk. A useful website that lists individual stock's correlation with the market is portfoliovisualizer.com.

CONCLUSION

Both setting up initially and actively managing an investment portfolio does take work and discipline. Your asset mix range weights in addition to your equity sector weights and individual stock, bond and ETF selections are critical. They determine the overall returns you can expect and how much volatility of returns that can be anticipated. Limiting your initial stock purchases to a maximum of 3-5% of all your stock holdings ensures that your returns will not be dramatically altered by the returns of one stock. In addition, trimming some stock positions periodically when their percentage weight exceeds 10% is a good risk-reducing policy to follow.

Adding up all your investments from all of your accounts creates a consolidated look at your asset mix and the risk levels assumed. This should be done at least quarterly if not more often to ensure you remain on the right track to achieve your long- term objectives.

This process also involves a detailed analysis of your mutual funds and ETFs, as many funds have very different asset mixes and equity and fixed income exposure than is readily apparent upon an initial glance.

Once you do this exercise routinely, you will become much more comfortable taking on a more active role in your investment decisions.

Now that you are more comfortable managing an investment portfolio, you are about to see how to read and interpret financial statements of companies.

CHAPTER 8
UNDERSTANDING FINANCIAL STATEMENTS

Many investors who are not trained in finance are terrified to even attempt to read a financial statement. Taking into account the investments you are making, it is a very good idea to familiarize yourself with the basics of accounting and financial statement disclosure. I have personally run across several investment counsellors who never read company quarterly and annual reports, opting instead to rely on the brokerage community exclusively for their research. I don't recommend this approach, as broker research is often biased and clouded by their investment dealer relationships with companies that need to issue additional capital.

This chapter offers you some insights into financial statement reporting. Under no circumstances should you assume that this is all you need to know. The subject is endless and accountants spend countless hours coming up with better disclosure requirements. I have gathered here some useful tips that may make your research both more enjoyable and useful in your investment decisions. Although I am not an accountant, both my practical experience managing money and my Chartered Financial Analyst designation qualify me to provide the information to help you make informed investment decisions.

Many of you have heard the terms Fundamental Analysis and Technical Analysis. Fundamental Analysis involves the analysis of financial statements, while Technical Analysis deals exclusively with long term stock price movements. While I do look at a company's price chart, my main focus is on Fundamental Analysis.

There are four key financial statements in any business that you will need to be able to read and understand.

1. **1.** Income Statement
2. **2.** Balance Sheet
3. **3.** Cash Flow Statement
4. **4.** Statement of Retained Earnings

The Income Statement measures the profits of a business over a specific period such as quarterly and annually. It takes into account all revenues and expenses, including estimates of the amount of depreciation and amortization.

The Balance Sheet is taken at a specific point of time such as at both quarter and year end. It measures all the company's assets and debts. What is left over is referred as Shareholder's Equity.

The Cash Flow Statement or Changes in Financial Position measures the actual cash received in and the actual cash paid out during a set period such as quarterly and annually. Differing from the Income Statement, it excludes non-cash expenses like depreciation, amortization and accounting write-offs, in addition to non-cash revenues.

Lastly, the Retained Earnings Statement is a statement at a specific point of time such as at quarter and year end. This statement takes into account the net profits of a business and deducts dividends paid to shareholders. Dividends are paid out of a company's retained earnings and are not a tax-deductible expense.

I encourage all of you to download an annual report of a company where you will be able to review a company's financial statements. You will notice a section called Notes to Financial Statements. Do not ignore this, as it often includes valuable financial information about a company. For example, if a company decides to change its accounting policies in regards to depreciation, the effect on the income statement will be itemized in these notes. The Notes to Financial Statements tend to be quite lengthy but are worth careful reading. Some of the items may include changes in accounting policies, lawsuits and contingencies, revenue recognition policies, company risks, business segment data and business acquisitions. Similar to the fine print in a business contract, the Notes to Financial Statements contain valuable information for the investor.

The long-term trend in a company's fundamentals are the most important. This is why it is required to review multiple years of financial data for at least five years, not simply the most recent. Review both absolute and per share numbers where appropriate to take into account share dilution through new issues.

Upon examining the Income Statement, you will notice a term in the US called GAAP and Non-GAAP Earnings. This refers to Generally Accepted Accounting Principles. Domestically, Canadian companies use Adjusted and IFRS earnings, with the latter short for International Financial Reporting Standards.

Why is this level of detail so important? When you are comparing companies together, it is important to compare apples to apples. This is why you should use either all GAAP or IFRS in the US and Canada respectively, or all Non-GAAP or Adjusted in the US and Canada respectively.

Personally, I look at both but normally use Non-GAAP in the US and Adjusted in Canada. These stats try to eliminate all extraordinary or non-recurring items so that an investor has a clearer view of a company's future prospects. Non-recurring items are of limited help to show any long-term trends. Both GAAP and IFRS earnings include all non-recurring gains and losses and non-recurring income and expenses.

If you decide to use Non-GAAP and Adjusted Earnings, it is still important to review the Income Statement to determine line by line if the income or expense reported is actually non-recurring. If the item is actually non- recurring, it needs to be excluded from the earnings per share calculation.

Stock-based compensation expense is normally excluded in the earnings per share calculation using Non-GAAP or Adjusted Earnings per share. This deduction is questionable as it tends to be a recurring expense.

An investor can avoid some of these issues with earnings per share calculations by avoiding the Income Statement altogether and by substituting it with the Cash Flow Statement. The cash flow statement adds back all non-cash items. However, many non-cash expenses are recurring and thus should not be added back.

As no one method is perfect, I review all of them, and recommend that you do the same.

On the balance sheet of a company, there is an asset called Goodwill. This represents an intangible asset created when one company acquires another. It equals the difference between the purchase price and the fair market value of the assets acquired. Goodwill cannot be amortized or expensed using either GAAP or Non-GAAP accounting in the US. Consequently, management must annually review goodwill to determine if there is an impairment or asset write down required. If possible, try to invest in companies with low Goodwill and Intangible Assets relative to Total Assets.

The Cash Flow statement is not affected by changes in accounting and non-cash write offs. In this regard it is often considered a more accurate assessment of a company's profitability. The energy industry uses cash flow as opposed to earnings to make comparisons between companies.

Free Cash flow is a company's operating cash flow less capital expenditures. It measures how much cash is left in a company to buy back stock, increase dividends and make acquisitions.

The Retained Earnings Statement is the balancing one between the Income and Balance Sheet Statements. The actual calculation is to add the beginning balance for the period and adding both net income and new issue capital. The deductions include stock buybacks and dividends.

Financial Ratios

These calculations emanate from the financial statements. There are five main groups of ratios – Liquidity, Asset Turnover, Leverage, Profitability and Dividend Policy. It is important to keep in mind that the trend of all the ratios is the most important factor and not to get carried away by one single ratio. You can easily google how to calculate all these ratios.

A liquidity ratio used frequently is called the Current Ratio. It is calculated by taking a company's Current Assets and dividing them with Current Liabilities. A ratio significantly above 1 is one measure to indicate the immediate solvency of the company.

Accounts Receivable and Inventory Turnover Ratios indicate how many times during the period that these assets turn into cash. The higher the number the better.

Leverage ratios measure how much overall debt a company has relative to both their operating cash flow and owners' equity. A company with a high level of debt relative to both its equity and operating cash flow is exposing the investor to more risk. However, certain defensive industries like utilities and consumer staples tend to have higher debt levels compared to more cyclical ones. This is because their revenues, earnings and cash flows are more consistent and predictable.

Profitability ratios measure how profitable a company is relative to both their total assets and shareholders' equity. In addition, profit margins measure how profitable a company is on their core business revenues. Obviously higher margins are better than lower, but the trend in these ratios is even more important.

Dividend Policy ratios have been explained in another chapter of this book. What is important is not the actual dividend yield, but the amount of growth in the dividend over time. A low payout ratio combined with strong cash flow growth and an unleveraged balance sheet bode well for the sustainability of the dividend.

Financial Statement Red Flags

Upon reviewing a company's statements, you may see some issues that could be a concern for its future prospects. I call these red flags.

A company that continuously changes accounting policies or shows a high turnover of senior executives indicates a warning for investors. A company that registers a material reduction in annual capital expenditures and/or research and development costs without a proper explanation is to be flagged. Finally, a company that suddenly has very low inventory and accounts receivable turnover may be the first sign of problems with their revenues.

CONCLUSION

Understanding financial statements will help you achieve more consistent investment returns. Companies that show predictable growth in revenues, cash flow and earnings tend to perform well over time. A healthy balance sheet gives a company an advantage over one that is highly leveraged. Companies that can show strong organic growth in sales without having to make too many acquisitions usually provide solid investment returns.

However, there are some companies that rely exclusively on growing through acquisitions with a great deal of success. Thermo Fisher, the US healthcare company, historically has a very successful long term track record of making accretive acquisitions as shown by its remarkable share price performance over the last three years.

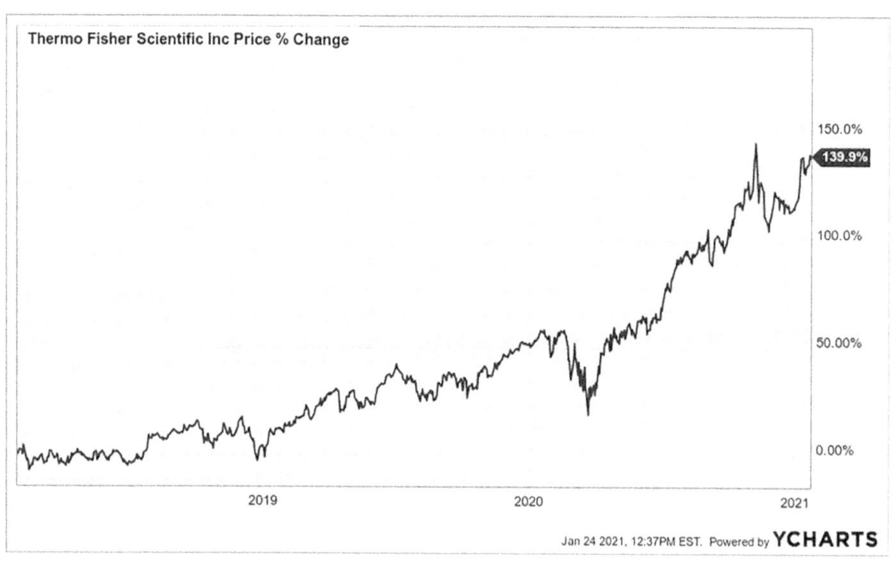

Thermo Fisher - price % change

Now that you are familiar with reading financial statements, you are about to learn the important factors in the stock selection process.

49

HOW TO PICK A STOCK FOR PURCHASE

Choosing individual stocks is only one part of the process. Both asset mix and equity sector selection are more important factors in terms of investment performance. However, stock picking remains an important element in any case. Differing from what many of you currently use in your stock selection process, I will provide you with the most relevant factors to improve your chances for success. I have spoken with many retail investors and asked them specifically what process they use to pick a stock. To my complete amazement, many investors only use the stock's absolute price momentum as their sole criteria. One gentleman indicated to me that he researches a stock's 52 week high-low price range and tries to choose a stock based on how close it is to the 52-week low price. Not only is this method not fundamental research, it is a form of bottom fishing that rarely works.

I realize that many of you do not feel financially savvy enough to read a financial statement and consequently relegate yourself to the share price only. In my opinion this is a dangerous strategy as it virtually ignores all the relevant facts of a company such as revenues, earnings, cash flow, debt/equity ratios and valuation measures based on these fundamental factors.

Type of Industry and Outlook

The first thing I look at when I do my research is to determine what industry the company is involved in and if the industry is categorized as cyclical, growth or defensive. Cyclical industries, like mining, energy and industrials and financials are much more affected by economic cycles than defensive consumer industries like grocery stores. Consequently, it is necessary to determine the cyclicality of its revenues and earnings. It is also key to assess if the economy is about to go into another recession or is rebounding from the last one. You really want to be careful investing a lot into cyclical companies in the middle of a recession, but you still want to own them coming out of one. Choosing an energy company based on its current dividend is not a good strategy to follow. Generally cyclical industries cut their dividends in an economic slowdown and only raise them again when the economy has already recovered.

For defensive industries like healthcare and consumer staples, the revenues and earnings are much more stable than in cyclical industries and thus the probability of a dividend cut is quite low. These defensive industries tend to have more debt as a percentage of equity since there is much less risk of default with the stability of revenues and earnings. For many cyclical industries that go in and out of profitability, I would not use the traditional valuation measure which is the Price / Earnings per share ratio (P/E).

Purchasing cyclical stocks when the P/E ratio is very high or infinity often works out, whereas buying when the P/E is very low historically does not work out. This is because the denominator of the ratio, namely the earnings per share, fluctuates from a loss to a profit. Purchasing a cyclical company when the P/E is low indicates that the earnings per share have probably peaked and will start going down. For cyclical companies I use other valuation measures like Enterprise Value to Projected EBITDA, Free Cash Flow Yield, Financial Debt to Trailing 12 month EBITDA and Price/ Book value. I also use projected EBITDA growth rates for these industries over the next few years. On the other hand, for defensive and growth companies, I use traditional valuation measures like the P/E ratio because a low ratio indicates the earnings are very low and may be troughing. This can normally be a good time to buy, but not always.

After reading this book, you will discover that there is not one single factor to use. There are many diverse measures to use that will improve your chances. It is also very important to keep in mind that the inherent high volatility of cyclical stocks do not make these companies ideal candidates for long term purchase. Investing in cyclical industries should be done when the economic cycle is expanding or about to recover and sold or reduced substantially at the onset of an economic recession. This rule applies specifically to industrial cyclicals like

Energy, Materials and Industrials. However, it also applies to consumer cyclicals like Consumer Discretionary and Financials.

Company's Fundamentals and Historical and Projected Growth rates

Reviewing a company's fundamentals is critical to determine the current prospects. Scanning through their quarterly and annual reports will give you many much needed facts. In order to eliminate any distortion from new share offerings, I look at both absolute and per share numbers for revenues, earnings, operating cash flow, book value and dividends. In addition I review quarterly and annual numbers both against their year over year results and against the consensus earnings per share and revenue estimates that are available on your discount broker website. For comparative purposes, I review a company's fundamentals on both a year over year quarterly basis and on a year over year trailing twelve-month basis (TTM). Percentage changes in the numbers are important as they can indicate both short and long- term growth trends. I also review operating and net margins to determine how much of a company's revenues are retained and to see how much operating and other costs are being kept under control.

Earnings before interest, taxes, depreciation, amortization (EBITDA) is a form of cash flow and is normally provided by companies in their financial reports. In addition to EBITDA, I also review a company's operating and free cash flow numbers. Operating cash flow is basically net income plus non-cash items like deprecation and amortization plus or minus any annual changes in non-cash working capital. Free cash flow is simply operating cash flow less capital expenditures. A company's free cash flow is what they have left in cash after that. It is the figure that can be used by a company to make additional acquisitions, make stock buybacks or increase the dividend. A company that has lots of free cash flow can expand organically without having to make more acquisitions. This is often a good indicator of a stronger company than one that needs to make acquisitions simply to grow. However, there are always exceptions to this rule.

The calculation of earnings per share is also up for interpretation. By reviewing quarterly financial statements, you will notice both GAAP and Non-GAAP

Earnings per share numbers in the US and IFRS and Adjusted Numbers in Canada. In the chapter titled *Understanding Financial Statements* these differences are explained in more detail. For simplicity purposes, either Non-GAAP or Adjusted Earnings per share refers to earnings before non-recurring extraordinary items. I look at both lines but concentrate on the earnings before non-recurring items. These are shown in Canada with the Adjusted Earnings per share number and in the US with the Non-GAAP one. However, it is important to keep in mind that many companies try to categorize any recurring expense item as "extraordinary" so their earnings look more favourable.

I always compare a company's fundamentals against three variables as follows:

- Relative to a company's history
- Relative to a company's peers in the same industry
- Relative to the overall market

In this way you can measure both the historical and projected growth rates of a company's fundamentals.

Return on equity is another important ratio. It measures how a company is doing relative to the book value of its equity. This ratio includes many factors including leverage, both accounts receivable, and inventory turnover. The turnover items refer to how many times every year inventory and accounts receivable turn into cash, with the more times the better.

Company's Market Valuation

There are many valuation measures being used today. I use all of them depending on the type of company and the type of industry. I use ratios such as the Price/ Earnings per share, Price/ Book value per share, Price / Cash Flow per share, Enterprise Value / EBITDA, Dividend yield, and Cash Dividend Payout. Note that the Enterprise Value refers to the market capitalization of the stock's common and preferred shares plus the company's bonds outstanding. When looking at these valuation measures, please remember that any ratio needs to be taken in perspective to be of any real use.

Company's Financial Condition

Another critical factor to be aware of is the company's financial health. This is especially important in an economic downturn. I use several ratios to measure a company's strength as follows:

1. Long-term debt / shareholder's equity measures the amount of leverage a company has at any point of time.

2. Another effective ratio I use is Financial Debt / EBITDA. According to Ycharts, Financial Debt consists of non-operational debt the company has. It includes accounts payable but not notes payable.

3. Times/Interest earned is another ratio of financial strength that measures the number of times, during the period measured, that EBITDA covers the interest expenses.

4. A company's working capital ratio measures current assets relative to current liabilities. This ratio indicates a company's immediate solvency.

The two attached graphs clearly show the fundamental deterioration in Sears Holdings, in terms of both their overall debt levels and the collapse in EBITDA.

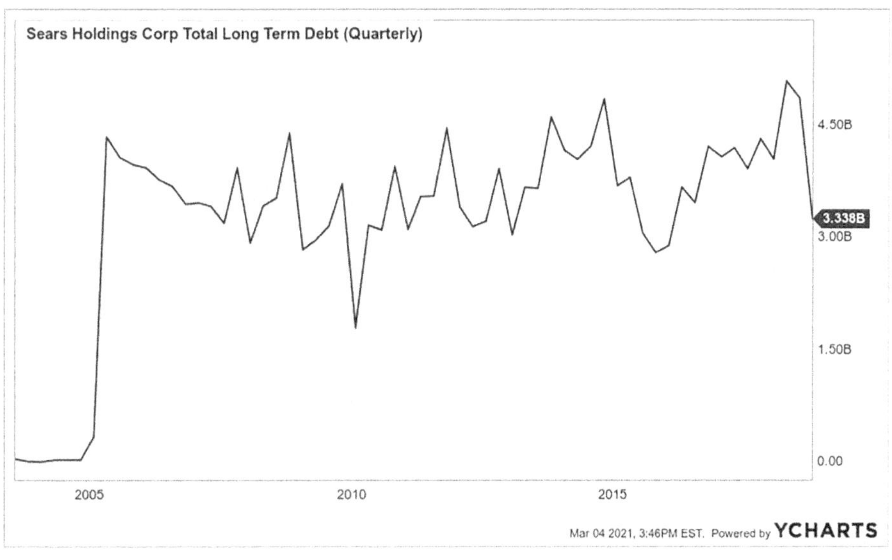

Sears Holdings - Total Long Term Debt

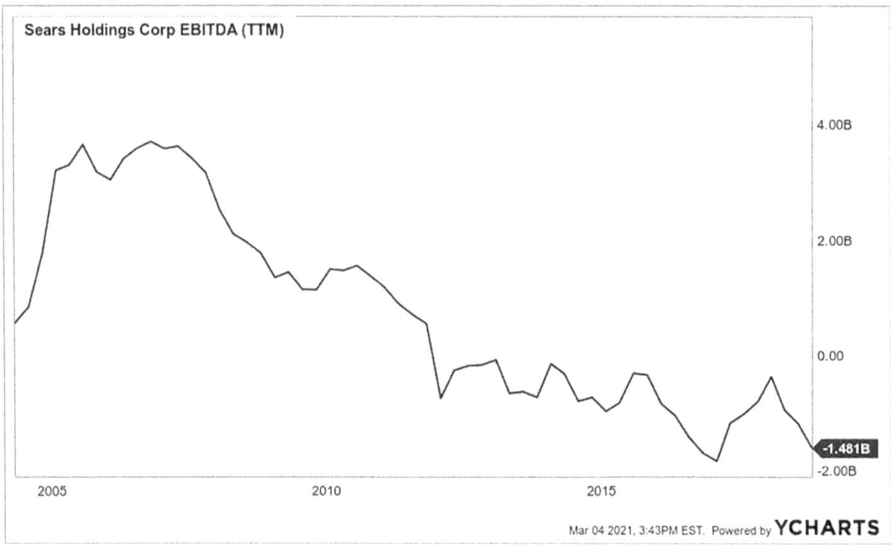

Sears Holdings - EBITDA

Company's Fundamental Outlook

Analyzing every company's future prospects accurately in detail is very time-consuming. I save time by using a consensus of earnings, revenues and EBITDA numbers, if available, for a company's prospects. These projections can be found in many places, including the research provided on your discount brokerage site selected. I also go to Ycharts online for this information, but it is a professional paid subscription service. You may not need that level of engagement. Zacks, the US consensus earnings database is also available for both US and inter-listed Canadian companies.

After gathering these projections for the next several years, you can then assess a company's annual growth prospects in relation to their market valuation. This is called the PEG ratio. It is a company's P/E divided by the growth rate of the earnings per share. Like most other ratios, there are different ways to calculate the number. Some analysts use historical earnings per share growth rates, while others use projected growth rates. I prefer using the projected growth rates as it more closely reflects a company's future prospects. In addition, you can use the Projected P/E multiple, and not the one using twelve months trailing earnings per share, in this calculation. This ratio is very useful as it ranks all companies against their growth rates. For fast growing companies with high P/E valuations, the PEG ratio puts everything into perspective.

I also recommend that you review a company's annual and quarterly management's outlook as well as recent news. You will see if a company is expanding or contracting and learn how company management is handling the current environment. This information is vitally useful to you as an investor.

Technical Analysis of a company's share price

Your focus on picking a stock is not solely dependent on looking at the share price. However, you may benefit from taking a glance at a company's share price in relation to the following criteria:

1. Is the share price trading above its 50- and 200-day moving average price? This normally indicates the shares are in an uptrend.

2. Is the percentage change in the share price in a rising trend? This refers to the slope of the line, with the higher the better. This percentage change is referred to as the stock's relative strength.

3. How is the share price doing relative to both the market and its competitors in the same industry? If the stock is doing better on a relative basis, this is a good thing.

Insider Trading

It is of interest to also look at insider trading, but this information is far more important for a smaller company than for a larger one. There are many reasons why an insider sells some stock, but normally only one reason that propels them to buy. The reason insiders buy small cap stocks is normally as a result that something positive about the company is about to happen.

CONCLUSION

Apart from technical analysis and insider trading, your main focus in assessing a company's future prospects involves fundamental factors affecting both the industry a company operates in and the specific revenues and earnings prospects of each company. The stock's market valuation in relation to its earnings growth prospects is always an important consideration.

If you take a company and compare it to its peers in the same industry using all the above criteria you will have a much clearer understanding of all the factors involved. This method helps you assess how the company selected is performing currently and how it is expected to perform in the future.

Now that you know some of the factors in the stock selection process, you are about to see even more factors for your selection of dividend paying securities.

CHAPTER 10
HOW TO INVEST IN DIVIDEND-PAYING STOCKS

In this chapter you will learn the important factors to consider when selecting dividend paying stocks for your portfolio. You will clearly see that picking the highest yielding stocks as the only criteria is not a good strategy to follow. Investing in companies with strong balance sheets that have stable to rising operating cash flows and low dividend payouts is the way to invest your capital. Companies that consistently increase their dividends annually are good purchase candidates. While there are exceptions, investing in companies in cyclical industries for the dividend only should be kept to a minimum, as these dividends could be slashed in an economic recession.

Many income-oriented investors only invest in companies with high dividend yields thinking that this strategy will satisfy their investment goals. As well, there are many mutual and exchange traded funds that also invest with the same objective. Unfortunately, many companies in cyclical industries like energy, mining and industrials have no qualms about cutting their dividends when times get tough. When this occurs, investors end up with a capital loss combined with a much lower dividend than they originally expected.

Normally, companies with unusually high dividend yields that are much greater than their peers are in financial difficulty and need to attract capital. In some instances, these companies have not yet cut the dividend but are on the verge of doing so.

Whether you invest in high yielding securities that are about to cut the dividend or those where they have no intention of increasing their dividends, it really does not matter. I do not recommend either option.

As an example, let's compare the historical returns of two Canadian energy companies – Vermilion Energy and Canadian Natural Resources. In May, 2019 Vermilion offered a dividend yield of 9.56% while Canadian Natural shares were yielding around 3.96%. Many investors flocked to Vermilion's common stock, only to be very disappointed less than a year later. The company initially cut its dividend per share in half in early 2020, then shortly after eliminated their dividend altogether. On the other hand, the lower yielding Canadian Natural maintained its quarterly dividend. For the last three years ending January 22nd of this year, the total return of Vermilion Energy was a negative 44.47% vs. a loss of 6.83% for Canadian Natural Resources. I have also included a graph on the share price percentage change for both companies over the last three years. The difference is even more striking with Vermilion's share price falling 86% and Canadian Natural only 31%. This example shows that investing only in high yielding stocks may not always be the best strategy.

Vermilion Energy vs. Canadian Natural Resources - % change in share price for the last 3 years

In creating a dividend investing policy, it is essential to look at many factors with the actual dividend yield the least important. Companies that increase their dividends annually are my preferred candidates for investment compared to those that rarely increase their dividends.

Making sure your investment returns keep up with the annual cost of living is a very important factor that many investors ignore. The objective is to ensure that your investment income should maintain its purchasing power as inflation rises every year. If your income does not keep pace with inflation, your standard of living will decline over time. In this example, assume your investments generated an annual income after tax of $30,000. This amount could have bought you a new car in 2020. However, if inflation goes up by 2.5% annually for five years, that same $30,000 will not buy you one new car in the year 2025 as the price of the car would have risen to $33,942.

Tax Efficiency of Canadian Dividends

A great deal of research clearly shows the tax benefits of the Canadian dividend tax credit for investments held in non-registered accounts. (This does not apply to Tax Free Savings accounts where there are no tax implications.)

In Canada both common and preferred dividends are eligible for the tax credit. Regardless of the tax benefit, it is still essential to choose your dividend-paying securities carefully. It is not wise to choose tax minimization as your reason to invest in a security. I have seen many instances in my past life as a portfolio manager when investors focused only on saving taxes, only to be disappointed later with their investment returns from that security. Accountants frequently come up with investments designed to save taxes, but, more often than not, these investments turn out to be duds in terms of investment performance and they exhibit a lack of marketability.

Analysis of Company's Fundamentals

Before investing in any company, it is important to review the company's fundamentals that are clearly summarized in the financial statements. For dividend-paying stocks, pay specific attention to both the balance sheet and the cash flow statement.

The balance sheet shows how much working capital (current assets less current liabilities) and the amount of long-term debt and liabilities relative to shareholder's equity. A company with too much debt relative to equity and relative to EBITDA is a definite red flag in making your purchase choices. Companies in certain defensive industries like utilities carry more long-term debt as a percentage of equity than other industries do. This is due principally to their more stable revenues and earnings and is not a sign of weakness. However, companies in cyclical industries like energy, mining and industrials have more erratic revenue and earnings streams. Consequently, these cyclical companies that have a more leveraged balance sheet are more vulnerable in an economic recession to cut their dividends to preserve cash and liquidity.

While the income statement is a non-cash reflection of a company's profitability, the cash flow statement more clearly highlights how much cash the company is generating. Despite seeming counter-intuitive, many companies borrow to pay their dividend and this trend applies to both small cap and large cap companies. Operating cash flow is calculated by adding all non-cash items to net income and adjusting for any changes in non-cash working capital. The ratio of financial debt to EBITDA (earnings before interest, taxes, depreciation, and amortization) is a hybrid calculation that measures the amount of debt relative to a version of operating cash flow. A higher ratio well above 1 time could be a sign of financial problems, but it largely depends on the cyclicality of the industry.

Free cash flow is an even better way to assess a company's probability of either increasing or cutting its dividend. Free cash flow is what a company has left over after paying its capital expenditures and preferred dividends. This amount is frequently used by companies to increase their dividends, make stock buybacks and new acquisitions.

Many companies have negative cash flows, but continue paying their dividends from borrowed capital. This is clearly not a good strategy and is not sustainable.

Investing in companies that have a low to moderate dividend payout ratio is important in determining if a company can sustain its dividend or increase it. While there are different ways to calculate this payout ratio, I use the following formula: Common dividends paid / operating cash flow less capital expenditures and preferred dividends.

The Real Estate Investment Trust Industry (REIT) uses a non-GAAP accounting term called Funds from Operations to calculate their dividend payout. This is determined by adding Net Earnings plus Depreciation and Amortization and then subtracting capital gains on the sales of properties. Please note that the calculation does not take new purchases of properties into consideration.

Once the Funds from Operations (FFO) is determined, REIT'S divide their current dividends per share into FFO per share. The result is the industry standard dividend payout ratio.

When analyzing one company compared to another in a different industry, it is important to make sure you are comparing apples to apples. Otherwise the comparisons are not useful.

CONCLUSION AND RECOMMENDATION

Investing in financially strong companies with solid balance sheets that regularly increase their quarterly dividends per share is a much better strategy than only picking the highest yielding securities. In addition, preferred buy candidates are companies that have growing operating cash flows and reasonable dividend payouts.

Companies that generate positive free cash flows are more likely to grow their dividends over time and less likely to cut their dividends. These are the factors that help to ensure that your income maintains its purchasing power over time.

While there are exceptions to every rule, companies in stable non-cyclical industries can have more leveraged balance sheets than cyclical ones without any fear of a dividend cut. Investing in cyclical industries for the dividend yield is a high-risk strategy where you can expect a dividend cut during an economic downturn.

Never choose tax minimization strategies to select your dividend securities as accountants are not known for their savvy investment recommendations.

Now that you are more familiar with the important factors in selecting dividend paying securities, you are about to learn how to enhance your net worth by investing in long term secular growth themes.

CHAPTER 11
RIDING LONG TERM INVESTMENT THEMES

It is important to always keep the current secular (long term) themes into account in your investment decisions. Even though I recommend a diversified portfolio with equity exposure in all sectors, investing in sectors that exhibit secular growth is essential so your retirement funds may prosper. The recent Covid-19 pandemic has brought these themes more into the spotlight. E-commerce, digital advertising, corporate migration to the cloud, video conferencing, wireless 5G implementation, video streaming, electronic gaming and sports and tele-health are just a few examples of these trends.

Technology

Long before the Covid-19 pandemic began, several trends developed to lower the costs for consumers. Air BNB and Uber were both established to offer a more competitive price experience when travelling and commuting. Amazon and its E-Commerce efforts had totally transformed the way many of us buy products. Digital advertising had virtually replaced print advertising leaving many newspaper companies fighting for their survival. Traditional bricks and mortar retailers had been forced to provide an online alternative or face bankruptcy. Retailers like Wal-Mart, Costco and Target were able to compete against Amazon only because they spent large sums on technology upgrading their on-line presences to levels comparable to Amazon. Shopify, our domestic high tech darling, has offered both small, mid and large businesses the ability to sell their products and services digitally. This has resulted in thousands of small businesses being created where people can work from home and yet attract buyers from all over the world. Many fintech software companies have greatly helped the large financial institutions improve the consumers' online accessibility to all the bank's products and services.

These trends in technology are not cyclical, but involve a long-term secular shift in how our economy functions. Companies like Facebook and Google dominate digital advertising to the frustration of many large companies who prefer more options. Whether we personally like or dislike these two online advertisers, there is little choice for most small business owners. In the corporate enterprise switch to the online cloud services, there are three companies that dominate this space.

Amazon, Microsoft and Google dominate, with Amazon the clear leader. Despite its leadership in e-commerce, Amazon derives the bulk of their revenues and earnings from cloud computing. In the online sports and gaming area, Activision Blizzard and Electronic Arts are the major players in North America. The global switch from the current wireless 4G technology to 5G will be a major technological innovation. In fact, the wireless transition to 5G is just in its early stages and will lead to much more content and speed available on our cellphones. Companies like Cisco and Qualcomm will be major forces in the 5G space. Video streaming has increased very rapidly in the pandemic and this trend is coming from all providers, including Apple, Disney, Comcast and Netflix. Video teleconferencing from companies like Microsoft and Zoom are permanently changing the way businesses carry on their activities and these trends are expected to negatively affect the travel industry. While consumer travel is expected to recover once the pandemic eventually subsides, business travel is not likely to recover to what is was before the pandemic.

Renewable Energy

The switch from traditional hydrocarbons to renewable energy is ongoing and is permanently changing the landscape of energy supply. At current prices renewable energy is very price-competitive relative to hydrocarbons and this is without any subsidies. As we all know, fossil fuels are not good for the environment and groups all over the world are protesting against its ill effects. Norway's sovereign wealth fund has recently sold most of their fossil fuel investments in protest to the environmental concerns. Many large industrial warehouses are converting from fossil fuel supply to renewable energy. This industry consists of companies involved in hydro, wind, solar and geothermal. Biomass, derived from both living organisms and through co-generation of pulp and paper waste, is another very important component of this renewable industry.

The renewable energy industry is in a long-term secular growth trend and, differing from the fossil fuel industry, is not a cyclical one. We all know that industries in secular uptrends tend to outperform stock market benchmark indexes over time. The fastest growing source of renewable energy globally is wind with solar a close second.

In the future, renewable energy will be providing most of the electricity for heating homes, plants and warehouses. While this will take time, it will happen. Despite our country's preoccupation with fossil fuels, the real growth will be derived from renewables. A recent law was just passed in France mandating all new roofs of commercial buildings must be covered either in plants or solar panels.

A great many companies are involved in renewable energy. Domestic companies like Algonquin Power continue to register strong investment returns relative to the overall market with their ongoing growth prospects. Other companies involved in this industry include US NextEra Energy that owns a majority stake in the largest renewable energy company in the US. European companies have led the industry globally in terms of new projects, while the US clearly needs to play catch-up from their current position. The reluctance of Americans to be first in this industry can be largely attributed to Trump and his preference for hydrocarbons. The recent election of Joe Biden and the Democrats will accelerate America's switch to renewable energy.

Health Care Industry

The demographic of our aging global population is creating an increase in demand for health care services of all types, including new drugs, actual health care of patients, medical devices and medical insurance. Covid-19 has dramatically sped up the need for vaccines and anti-viral medications to stop the progression of this pandemic. We have been made painfully aware of the lack of proper health care in the US for 40 million plus Americans. This pandemic has resulted in a much higher incidence in the black, Hispanic, and low income populations of the US of both contracting Covid and dying. This is absolutely disgraceful for a wealthy country like the US to treat their poor and downtrodden so terribly. Fortunately, we can expect a very different approach from Biden and the Democrats in this regard.

The global market for diabetes drugs and devices is expected to grow to $111.2 billion by 2027, expanding at a compound annual growth rate of 3.9%. In addition to the products and services already mentioned above, there are many companies involved in tele-health, a relatively new industry that uses digital information via laptops and mobile devices to access health care services remotely. Mobile devices, including Apple now have an app to inform all the close contacts of someone recently infected with Covid, to ensure that they self-quarantine.

There are many choices when investing in the health care industry. There will always be winners and losers but the industry as a whole is in a long-term growth trend spurred on by innovation, public health needs, and our aging population. Bristol Myers, Abbvie, Pfizer and Johnson & Johnson are four examples of companies in this industry.

Eletrification of Vehicules

Most industry specialists believe that the switch from cars and trucks being powered from hydrocarbons to battery powered electricity will all be completed within the next 5-8 years, if not earlier. This is clearly a long term secular trend. While Tesla is the dominant player in this transition so far, VW and General Motors are not far behind. My investor preference is GM and the Canadian auto parts company, Magna International.

CONCLUSION

Always keep your eyes open for long term, non-cyclical trends. These are relatively easy to spot, but you need to be acutely aware of them in order to use them for your investment ideas. Technology, Renewable Energy, Health Care and the Electrification of Vehicles are four of the current trends. Also, take notice not only of the distinct difference between a short-term cyclical pickup in certain industries such as Industrials and Materials, but also note their long term more permanent trends.

Now that you are more familiar with many of the current long term secular growth themes, you are about to learn the importance of investing in gold and gold shares.

CHAPTER 12
INVESTING IN GOLD, SILVER AND COPPER

In August of last year, gold bullion reached an all time high of $2067 US per ounce before falling back down to the current level of $1729 as of the end of February, 2021. Apart from the recent pullback, gold has benefitted from low nominal interest rates in addition to negative real rates and a sharply increasing global money supply. Another tailwind for gold over the last several years has been the weak US dollar relative to most international currencies in addition to the increase in trade tensions between the US and China under the Trump Administration.

Gold has been seen as a store of value and a viable substitute for paper currencies. The demand for jewellery, especially in countries like India, provides long term demand for gold. Historically gold has risen during periods of economic stress and political unrest. Gold has been a hedge against both inflation and surprisingly in some circumstances, deflation.

For the last five- and ten-year periods, concluding the end of February, 2021, gold bullion has sharply underperformed the US Standard & Poor's equity index. Gold shares as measured by the US GDX ETF, have also fared worse than the US equity market over these same periods. However, over the last five years gold shares' performance has only been marginally lower than the US equity market. It is important to keep in mind that investing in gold bullion does not yield a dividend like investing in the stock market does. While it is difficult to predict future price trends, it is nevertheless important to analyze the reasons for the recent performance to see if it is likely to continue.

Normally there is a divergence in price between the actual bullion and gold companies' share prices. This is because every company has unique strengths and weaknesses that have nothing to do with gold bullion. We have all probably heard the term "price leverage". This means that if gold bullion rises by 10%, the benefit to a gold producer's operating cash flow is enhanced by a factor more than 1 for 1. Taking into consideration that unit costs remain relatively flat over a short period of time, any marginal price improvement in the commodity goes directly to the bottom line without any change in unit costs. Consequently, operating margins rise by more than the 10% increase in bullion prices. Despite all of this it is still important to keep in mind that price leverage moves in both directions, positive and negative. As well, much depends on the quality of the company, its ore grade and its ability to control its operating costs.

The level and direction of nominal interest rates play an important role in the outlook for gold bullion. The very large monetary stimuli provided by all the world's central banks have led to this current low-rate environment. As gold bullion offers no yield, higher interest rates pose a competitive threat owning gold.

Real interest rates are another critical factor in determining where gold prices are heading. These represent nominal rates less the cost of inflation. Historically gold prices move up sharply when real rates turn negative. Gold and real yields tend to move in opposite direction. They have a negative correlation with each other.

The relative weakness of the US dollar globally over the last several years has also acted as a tailwind for gold bullion prices. However, should the US dollar reverse its course and start to exhibit strength globally, this would be a negative for gold prices.

Investors wanting to participate in the global economic recovery may want to consider both silver and copper as alternatives to gold. Both metals are more industrial commodities than gold and are more affected by the global supply / demand situation for each respective commodity. The global switch to renewable energy is expected to see strong growth for both copper and silver. The electrification of vehicles is seeing ever-increasing demand for both metals. Currently 10% of the global silver supply is used to make solar panels.

CONCLUSION

Both nominal and real interest rates will continue to play an important role in the direction of gold prices. In addition, the direction of the US dollar globally has a short-term effect on gold prices.

In the US, nominal interest rates are just beginning to climb back up. As well, real interest rates, which remain negative, are turning less negative for the first time. These are both negative trends for gold bullion prices. As the economic recovery unfolds, interest rates cannot remain at these current low levels.

The outlook for both silver and copper is more favourable than gold at this time. Pan American Silver is a Canadian silver producer and Capstone Mining is a Canadian copper producer. Personally, I prefer investing in the actual companies as opposed to the commodity.

Although I prefer silver and copper producers to gold ones at this time, I am not against investing in a high-quality Canadian gold producer like Agnico Eagle.

Now that you have learned how to invest in gold, silver and copper, you are about to learn how personal biases negatively affect your net worth.

CHAPTER 13
INVESTMENTS AND PERSONAL BIAS

As human beings we all have phobias and biases that we try to hide under the carpet and forget they exist. But it is much healthier admitting our weaknesses to ourselves. It may even make us richer financially knowing exactly what they are.

This chapter is exclusively devoted to biases that can negatively affect our financial net worth. The following are only a few examples. The list is endless.

Do not own common stocks for fear of losing money

I know may people who will not ever purchase a common stock. This is amusing to me as most of these individuals hold mutual funds that consist mainly of common stocks. One person I know bought one speculative stock years ago that was recommended by a friend. Unfortunately, she lost a sizeable amount of money and decided from that point on never to buy a stock again. In her case, she does not even own equity mutual funds or ETFs. Her rationale is that stocks are far too risky and she cannot afford to lose any capital. These seem like logical explanations, but her decision has negatively affected her net worth and financial well being.

She prefers to invest exclusively in bank GICs, savings accounts and money market funds that unfortunately provide her with very little return. I have told her on many occasions that her capital would have been far better invested purchasing her bank's common stock rather than the bank's products.

Invest 100% of portfolio in stocks for fear of being left behind

Many investors of all ages routinely invest all their assets in common stocks. Their logic is that market timing does not work and stocks always perform well over the long run. However, having cash in a volatile market is normally a good strategy and helps to significantly reduce portfolio volatility, especially in a bear market.

Equity Sector Bias

Many investors who either work in high tech or invested in the industry in the past, have developed an investor bias never to buy these type of stocks again.

Once again, their explanation sounds logical, but it really is totally irrational. Technological innovations provide the growth engines for our global economy and investing in this sector over time has provided some of the best investment returns in the stock market.

On the other hand, some investors prefer to restrict their investments to industries where they work. This also seems to make sense as their level of familiarity with industry best practices is the highest. However, investing in one industry lacks sufficient diversification and significantly increases portfolio volatility. Even Bill Gates, the billionaire co-founder of Microsoft, invests in a wide diverse group of industries.

Do not like a company's products

Some investors are suspicious of the quality of certain retailers' products. However, many of these retailers have done very well, regardless of the quality of their products.

Do not use the product or service

Some investors do not like using social media. However, Facebook and Google have been great investments and will continue to be despite their recent setbacks with data breaches. Anyone operating a small business knows how valuable both Facebook and Google are in terms of marketing their products.

Fear of triggering a taxable capital gain

As an investment portfolio manager, I came across many clients who absolutely refused to sell a stock with a large unrealized capital gain in a taxable account.

In many cases, this one stock may have represented a very high percentage of their total equity exposure and added much more portfolio volatility than appropriate.

One of my former clients owned a very large position in Nortel. Every time I suggested reducing the position, he rejected my advice based solely on the tax consequences. We all know what happened to Nortel.

When Nortel was trading at its peak, this client had a sizeable net worth. Unfortunately, he chose to not sell the majority of his Nortel stock and this resulted in a material reduction in his family's financial well being.

Political Bias affecting your investment decisions

In the ever-omnipresent world of politics, this type of bias is becoming more common. The US population has never been more polarized over their political allegiances. The US has always been more political than Canada but today it is even more apparent. Many of us now judge others by their political allegiances. To judge someone negatively by who they vote for is very dangerous. This is a type of prejudice that harms society as a whole and pigeonholes specific groups to contrast with each other. For a harmonized society it is important and necessary to find ways to co-operate with each other. This is the only way to make us better.

Some investors foolishly sold all their equity investments as a result of political uncertainty with Trump when he was first elected. I do understand their anxieties but basing their whole financial net worth on a politician they do not approve of is not prudent business practice. A much better approach is to manage your investments around whoever is in power no matter what your political views are.

Religious or Ethical Bias

Some individuals prefer to invest only in areas that concur with their ethical and/ or religious beliefs. In most cases this type of investing does not enhance your net worth. Investors should never restrict their investments in this way, but it is done all the time.

CONCLUSION

Biases and prejudices get in the way of making good investment decisions. It is beneficial for each of us to identify what they are before we can manage our investments effectively.

Now that you have learned how personal biases can negatively affect your capital, you are about to read about some valuable lessons that I have learned in my working life that can be of great help in managing your portfolios.

CHAPTER 14
VALUABLE LESSONS I HAVE LEARNED INVESTING MY CAPITAL

Don't think that financial advisors always have your best interest at heart ahead of their own financial ones.

We all make mistakes that could have been avoided if we knew in advance what to do. As this is really not possible, what matters is that we learn valuable lessons to make sure we never make those same mistakes again.

In this chapter I have accumulated a long list of what to do and what not to do under certain circumstances.

The single most important message I want to relate is that investing needs to be done slowly and methodically. Make a lot of small bets as opposed to one or two large ones. Your long-term goal is to have a well-diversified portfolio that provides a rising dividend stream over time as a hedge against inflation. Try to limit how much you invest in any one company, industry and individual corporate bond to limit your risk. Consistency of investment returns is much better than a more volatile approach as you never know in the future exactly when you may need some of your capital in an emergency. Trying to sell securities when their valuations are down materially does long term damage to your net worth.

Asset mix and equity sector selection are more important factors than stock picking in determining your investment returns.

Try to do your own investment research rather than relying on others for their opinions. Spend more time analyzing an industry than on the analysis of an individual company in that industry.

When you purchase a bond or fixed income mutual fund or ETF, don't simply look at the current or distribution yield. Look at the yield to maturity. This takes into account both the current yield plus or minus the capital gain if you purchase a bond at either a premium or a discount to par value.

When you are choosing a short term, under one year, investment in an ETF or fund, make sure you consider the annual management fee before purchase. Also, keep in mind that there is no CDIC insurance for a fixed income mutual or exchange traded fund.

Unless you are absolutely sure of a stock, do not average down by purchasing more at a lower price than your original one. This strategy increases your overall risk by having an even larger weight in a stock that is going down in price. A good company does not always equate to a great stock investment.

Investing in a high Price/ Earnings per share ratio (PE) stock can be risky for two reasons:

1. If the company reports a poor earnings quarter that disappoints investors, the PE ratio can fall sharply, causing the shares to decline.

2. The share price can simply fall from the lower earnings.

Do not use stock screens as different industries use completely different variables. Thus, it is hard to compare one company in one industry to another company in another sector. Every industry uses unique measures that differ materially from other industries. For example, the energy industry prefers operating cash flow as opposed to net earnings to compare one company with another. This is because the non-cash expenses, deprecation and depletion, are a larger component of their overall expenses than many other sectors. Cash flow provides a more useful measure for commodity companies including base metal mining ones. In the REIT industry both net asset values and cap rates are used extensively. The cap rate is the reverse of the P/ E multiple, while the calculation of net asset value takes all the current market value of the properties less the total debts. Banks use the price / book value in addition to the P/E ratio for valuation purposes. In addition, other critical ratios include the percentage of non-performing loans to total loans and the corresponding percentage of reserve provisions against the total non-performing loans outstanding. In the construction and engineering industries, order backlog is considered one of the most important factors. This ratio is calculated by summing up all orders that have been booked but not yet shipped and delivered. These are only a few examples of the difficulty of comparing companies in different industries.

When you are doing your stock research, keep in mind that organic sales growth is normally better than growth from acquisitions.

An accretive acquisition is always preferred to a dilutive one. Normally this information is provided in a press release.

Do not always go for the maximum absolute price return when buying a stock. Pay attention to the risk you are taking in the security you choose. Consistency of returns is far better than high volatility.

Never buy a stock solely because you think it will be a takeover candidate. This rarely works out.

Do not make a decision on a company based on its share price only. A review of a company's fundamentals is usually the better strategy. Many people devote more time purchasing clothes or a computer than they do choosing their investments.

Bottom fishing is a term used by many investors who purchase companies that have recently seen their share price collapse. This strategy is high risk and is rarely a sure bet.

Try to distinguish between a turnaround stock and one that is a value trap. A value trap is a company that is historically very cheap, but cheap for a reason. A turnaround stock refers to a cyclical company that is expected to benefit from a rebound in economic growth.

Do not sell a stock simply because it has fallen in price. There are a multitude of reasons for the share price decline such as program trading that have nothing to do with a company's fundamentals.

Do not automatically sell a stock because insiders are liquidating some of their holdings. Insiders sell for many reasons, but usually buy for only one goal – to make a profit.

Never count on the dividend of a cyclical company as it could be cut anytime. Try not to invest in companies that borrow to pay their dividend.

Focus on companies that increase the dividend over time as opposed to ones with a high absolute dividend yield.

The outlook of an investment is far more important than the tax considerations. Many investors have paid a hefty price by keeping stocks with large unrealized capital gains for fear of paying the tax man.

Invest for the long term. Short term day trading is not a strategy that will consistently make you a lot of money as it is not based on a company's fundamentals.

Do not expect that all your investment choices will be winners. All of us lose money occasionally.

The concept of total return (dividend plus share price gains or losses) is a far more relevant concept in determining your investment performance than simply looking at either dividend yield or share price movements separately.

Most financial institutions charge anywhere from 1.5-2.5% to convert your Canadian monies to US and the same in reverse. If your investments are with a discount broker and you have a Canadian and US non-registered account, (not a TFSA), you can significantly reduce the foreign exchange fee by following a strategy called Norbet Gambit. Once you know exactly how much Canadian cash to convert into US dollars, call the trading desk of the discount broker and let them know exactly what you want to do. Simply mention the Norbet Gambit method and they will guide you through the process. Make sure you phone them. Do not do this online without speaking with someone first. You need to transact in an inter-listed security like the ETF DLR, a Canadian inter-listed security and DLR.U, an American inter-listed security. This strategy will save you a lot of money. I have used it myself and have been very happy with the result. You can also use this method to convert US dollars back into Canadian dollars with the same benefit.

On a short- term basis, a strong US dollar globally usually results in commodity prices going down. This is because most commodities, including crude oil, gold and base metals, are all traded in US dollars throughout the world. When the US dollar rises against foreign currencies, commodities become that much more expensive to a foreigner in their own currency. Consequently, demand falls and so does the price. I want to emphasize that this is only a short-term trend and many other factors play into the long- term outlook for commodities.

Financial companies' profitability improves when interest rates go up and deteriorates when rates decline. This is true for both banks and life insurance companies. Banks' operating margins, called net interest margins, rise when interest rates do as well. This is because banks borrow short-term funds and lend them out in longer term mortgages, earning a profit on the spread between the short and long rates. Insurance companies benefit from higher rates in that their long- term liabilities diminish in present value terms when interest rates are high. This concept is called the future and present value of money and this can be used for both assets and liabilities. For the insurance industry, I am only referring to the discounted value of the long-term liabilities.

Now that you have learned some valuable rules to enhance your net worth, you are about to see how your investing style should change at different stages in your life.

CHAPTER 15
INVESTING AT DIFFERENT STAGES IN YOUR LIFE

Many of us invest our hard-earned capital the same way we always have regardless of our age. In my opinion this is a major mistake. When you are young and starting out in your career you most likely do not have the same financial obligations as when you are older and own a home, a car and other assets, and have children. In addition, you can probably afford to lose some capital with many working years to make up the loss. On the other hand, retired people do not have the luxury of making back any losses with their working years behind them. As I have mentioned previously in this book, your asset mix is the single most significant factor in determining your investment performance. It is important to have different asset mixes at various stages of your life in order to meet your current objectives.

When you first start out in your career, your immediate need for income is minimal taking into account you have a salary. This stage of your life is called the accumulation phase. Income from your investments is not withdrawn but re-invested back into the security markets. Having a high equity weight is a good idea during this period of time, and you can take on more risk than later in your life. However, I would still like to highlight some issues that are relevant at this life's juncture. Many young investors like to gamble with their investments by purchasing low priced stocks that are highly volatile. Bottom fishing is the term used to describe some investors' preference to focus on poor quality companies whose share prices have fallen sharply. While I think that young investors can absorb more risk than retired investors can, I still do not advocate investing in poor quality investments at any age. There are always better alternatives that provide much more price upside with much less risk. My advice for young investors is to stick to quality companies but use a higher equity weight as your form of more risk.

Retired investors come in all forms. Some have a defined benefit pension plan that provides an indexed income for life. This income is in addition to the government's Canada Pension (CPP) and Old Age Security (OAS). Some may not have a full pension plan but rely on investments and CPP and OAS for retirement income. Some have a combination of the above.

Those with an indexed defined benefit pension can afford to take on more investment risk by having a higher equity weight. In this specific circumstance, the investment portfolio's objective can be more growth oriented as income needs are already being met from the pension.

For those without an indexed pension, the investment objective for an investment portfolio will need to be income with some limited capital growth to keep up with inflation. Maximizing income without any growth is not a good strategy either. Focusing on companies that increase their dividends is better than only investing in companies that offer a high dividend yield with limited future growth in the dividend. At this stage of life, capital preservation is very important. A retired investor cannot afford to speculate on risky securities. Having a higher cash weight in their investment portfolio is important to act as a buffer when equity markets go down. On the other hand, cash investments tend to yield very little and do not provide any inflation hedge.

For most retired investors, using investments to generate income is essential. However, at this stage of life they need to look at both the amount of the withdrawals from their portfolio in addition to the timing of those withdrawals. When you first retire, my recommendation is to maintain at least five years of your annual income requirements in cash. This is to avoid having to liquidate equities when they have declined in value during a market meltdown. For the remainder of your cash, you can set up a diversified investment portfolio consisting of both stocks and bonds that meets your income, growth and low risk requirements.

Now that you have seen how changing your investments at different stages of your life can be of financial benefit to you, you are about to see a summary of my objectives for writing this book.

CHAPTER 16
CONCLUSION

M any small investors have felt disenfranchised from large institutional money managers for a very long time. Several years ago there was a book published on black hole trading where actual details of trades were not disclosed to the retail public and were only privy to the large US banks and trading enterprises.

A recent episode involved small investors on the Robinhood trading app buying stocks like Gamestop and Blackberry, that had been heavily shorted by Wall Street hedge funds. This buying by small investors was to send the big money players a message that they can invest their money as well as the big hedge funds can. Unfortunately this did not work out very well for the small investor as the Robinhood platform was forced to follow regulatory compliance rules that limited the amount of trading by investors.

Hopefully my book will offer small investors the skills required to be able to compete effectively against the large institutional investors and help them to minimize excessive speculation and potential large capital losses.

My sole objective in writing this book is to provide you with the necessary tools to manage your own capital. The art of investment management is not rocket science, but does require hard work and discipline. It can be learned by anyone regardless of your level of financial knowledge. Please do not be persuaded by investment advisers who will try to discourage you in this pursuit. Many of these supposed experts have annual sales targets that drive their behavior much more than the investment performance of their clients. Take ownership of your financial affairs. You will not be disappointed. Once you take charge of your own investments and are in complete control, you will feel empowered.

RESOURCES

I refer to many sources of information as summarized below. One of the best sources is just to go online and google any financial subject. You will be surprised by what you find. It is important to keep in mind that many news channels, like Fox News, are politically biased.

These are the sources that I personally use on a regular basis. Once you get comfortable, you will tailor the sources you use to specifically satisfy your objectives. Some of you may only want to look at websites that address your income needs while others will focus on capital growth opportunities. You will need to keep in mind that if your ongoing research is not working well, you may want to review other possibilities. My book is all about you finding ways to increase your net worth. By keeping an open mind with how you invest will ultimately help achieve your long term goals.

1. *www.google.com* – The easiest way to answer any of your questions.
2. Value Line – You will need a library card to access online services. This is a paid subscription service that can be accessed for free by signing in to the Ottawa Library website and going to Online Resources. Value Line publishes a one- page report on all US companies and some Canadian inter-listed securities. You will need to input the stock's symbol and to scroll down to the bottom of the page where you will see a list and dates of the latest reports.
3. *www.ycharts.com* – This is a paid subscription service that I use to obtain detailed financial and economic information. It provides both the raw data in chart and table format. I find the service invaluable, but it is expensive. In my opinion, you get what you pay for.
4. *www.zacks.com* – This is a US service that is partially free and partially a paid subscription. The service provides consensus earnings estimates for US and some inter-listed Canadian companies.

5.   Discount Broker Investment Research Data – Most discount brokers offer a fair amount of investment research on both companies and industries. The research includes consensus earnings estimates as well.

6.   Individual Company Websites – If you are reviewing a company, go directly to the company website and click investor information. You will find plenty of interesting material including all quarterly and annual financial reports and all press releases.

7.   *www.sedar.com* – This is a website that also provides financial information on Canadian companies.

8.   *www.sedi.com* – This is a website offering insider trading activity for Canadian companies.

9.   *bankofcanada.ca* – Provides domestic economic statistics including foreign exchange and interest rates.

10.   *www.treasury.government/resource-center/data* – Provides US economic statistics.

11.   *www.yardeni.com* – Edward Yardeni is an American economist that provides an enormous amount of economic and financial information on both global economies and stock and bond market statistics. The timely statistics provided by this website are truly amazing and completely free of charge.

12.   *www.spglobal.com* – This site provides monthly updates on all global market indices including the TSX Composite and the S&P 500 Indices. The details include actual equity sector percentage weights.

13.   *www.kitcometals.com* – Provides recent price and inventory levels of commodities

14.   *www.eia.gov* – provides US energy reports

15.   *www.iea.com* – provides global energy reports

16.   *www.benefitscanada.com* –Provides a list of Canadian money managers. Once you have this list, you can go directly to several of their individual websites. Many of them offer complimentary quarterly newsletters where they highlight their outlook for security markets, equity sectors and specific stocks.

17.   *www.bnnbloomberg.ca* – Provides financial information, news and opinions on Canadian, US and global companies.

18.   *www.cnbc.com* – Provides financial information and news on global and domestic economic and individual company statistics.

19. Go onto the web and google specific industry information and outlook.

GLOSSARY OF TERMS

A glossary of the most important specific terms is included for your reference below.

Accretive Acquisition – When a company acquires another, if the benefit received to earnings or cash flow per share is greater than the percentage increase in shares outstanding, it is considered accretive.

Averaging Down – Refers to a strategy where an investor purchases more of the same stock at a lower price, thereby lowering the cost per share.

CDIC insurance – Canada Deposit Insurance Corporation – This is a crown corporation that insures the deposits of financial institutions.

DSC's or Deferred Sales Charges – These charges refer to fees the mutual fund company charges the investor to redeem their funds within a certain period of time.

EBITDA – Earnings before interest, taxes, depreciation and amortization

ETFs – Exchange Traded Funds – These are a much lower fee type of fund that only trades on the market like a stock.

High Yield Bonds – Refers to bonds that are not considered investment grade and that carry a higher risk.

MERs or Management Expense Ratio for a mutual fund – This refers to the costs of the fund to the investor with these costs being indicated on an annual basis in percentage terms.

PEG Ratio – refers to the PE multiple divided by the company's earnings growth rate

PE Multiple – Market Price of the stock divided by Earnings per share.

Rate Reset Preferreds – A type of preferred share that pays a fixed dividend rate for a period of five years, at which time the rate is reset to the five- year Government of Canada yield at that time plus a percentage spread over the Canada bond. Due to their reset nature, these type of preferreds perform much better when interest rates are rising and perform worse when they decline.

REITs – Real Estate Investment Trusts. These are trusts that differ from corporations in that they are required to distribute a large portion of their earnings to unitholders, thereby transferring the tax liability from the trust to the unitholders. These trusts invest in apartments, commercial and residential buildings, industrial warehouses, data centres, shopping malls and retirement homes. The trust is the landlord receiving rents and paying expenses.

Risk Adjusted Rate of Return – This term refers to measuring returns relative to the amount of risk assumed. For example, if you have two stocks with the same investment returns over a set period– one high risk and the other low risk. The higher risk security is not doing nearly as well as the lower risk one as a result of the much higher risk assumed.

Sector vs. Market Index ETFs – A market index ETF refers to an index fund representing the total market. A sector ETF refers to an equity ETF that invests only in one specific sector such as Financials.

Tactical vs. Strategic Asset Mix Strategies – Strategic asset mix refers to a long-term asset mix strategy, while tactical is a short- term strategy based on the market's current outlook.

Total Return – Dividend yield plus percentage change in share price

ACKNOWLEDGEMENTS

Let me start by thanking YCharts for their highly informative subscription service that provides very informative investment research and analysis.

I want to thank my friend, Richard Ruel, for continuously providing me helpful research and ideas for many years.

I want to thank Carol Sill, my editor, who has been instrumental in terms of her amazing feedback and ideas as well as her ongoing support. I could not have written the book without Carol.

I want to thank my graphic designer, Clémence Palvadeau, who has very artistically designed both my book's front and back covers and its contents.

I also want to thank my late parents, Shepherd and Dorothy McMurtry, my late sister Jill, my sister Anne, my uncle, Robert Walker, my two daughters, Lucy and Sarah, and my wife, Susan, for always believing in me and encouraging me to do my best and ensuring that I never forget that helping others is what it is all about.

ABOUT PETER MCMURTRY

Aformer work colleague recently asked me why I was writing this book after having worked in the industry for so long. My answer was simple. As I am no longer employed in the industry, I can offer my readers much more objectivity regarding the strengths and weaknesses of every aspect of this business. Investors really need to know these details before investing their life savings with someone they may not even know.

Since the late 1970's I have worked in the financial industry in various capacities including client service rep (broker), investment analyst, investment portfolio manager and in financial planning. For the past several years, I have written a monthly investment newsletter that provides both a strategy piece and two model portfolios. My Income and Growth Portfolios consist principally of individual stocks with some industry and region specific exchange traded funds. For my fixed income, I recommend exchange traded funds. I do not use mutual funds because of their higher cost structure.

My academic qualifications include a Bachelor of Commerce from McGill University and a Chartered Financial Analyst Designation, CFA, from University of Virginia.

I have managed both balanced and all equity portfolios. Both my practical experience and education provides me with the tools to make it much easier for investors to do the following:

- Analyze individual companies for both investment and disinvestment
- Analyze Equity sectors
- Set up and manage an investment portfolio
- Read and Interpret Company Financial Statements
- Proactively manage your portfolio's overall asset mix

My work experience includes working for banks and trust companies, investment dealers, in house pension funds, non-bank-owned investment counsellors and a financial planner. This gives me a broad perspective as to how the industry works and how investors can best position themselves.

For more information on my work and to subscribe to my monthly newsletter, please go to my website at *www.mcmurtryinvestmentreport.ca*.

Peter McMurtry, B.Com, CFA